M000164572

SACRED TEXTS

CELTIC WISDOM

Timeless Wisdom in
Poetry and Prose

Edited and Introduced by
Gerald Benedict

WATKINS PUBLISHING
LONDON

This anthology of Celtic poetry and prose has been
selected by Gerald Benedict

This edition produced in 2008 for Sacred Texts,
an imprint of Watkins Publishing
Sixth Floor, Castle House, 75–76 Wells Street, London W1T 3QH

1 3 5 7 9 10 8 6 4 2

Designed in Great Britain by Jerry Goldie

Typeset in Great Britain by Dorchester Typesetting Group
Printed and bound in Malaysia by Imago

British Library Cataloguing-in-Publication data available

ISBN: 978-1-905857-73-9

www.watkinspublishing.co.uk

CONTENTS

The mountains never meet, but people can always encounter each other.

Ancient Irish proverb

INTRODUCTION

People associated with the name Celt emerged from trans-European groups to be recorded as early as the 6th century BCE by Greek geographers and historians as the *Keltoi*. The name survived in the works of Latin writers as *Celtae,* and the Celts eventually emerged as a distinct people with their own varied forms of the parent Indo-European languages. The Celtic languages and dialects settled into two major linguistic divisions: Goidelic, or Gaelic, is associated with the Celtic Highlanders of Scotland, the Irish and the Manx; Brythonic, derived from the Welsh *Byrthon,* meaning an indigenous Briton, refers to the languages of Wales, Cornwall and ancient Cumbria. Breton, spoken by people of Brittany, is descended from the Brythonic branch of the language. Galicia, in north-western Spain, is unlike other regions of that country, being characterized by its Celtic inheritance and a dialect derived from Gaelic. Sadly, these Celtic languages are now spoken only in minority communities, but there are strong initiatives to revitalize the four main groups: Irish Gaelic, Scottish Gaelic, Welsh and Breton, together with Cornish and Manx. Celtic literature in English, for example Anglo-Irish, began at different times in the histories of these respective groups, each creating a tradition of its own. It is the stories told in these languages – of ancient myths, of nature full of mystery and magic, of heroes and heroines, of fairies and fabled seers, of gods both pagan and Christian, of Druids and the Celtic Christian saints – that lend their themes to a unique literature. Its poetic form is given what amounts to a sacred status, its composition and recitation offered as if it were a sacrament, the poets revered as if they were saints.

A resurgent 19th-century interest in Celtic culture set out to rediscover the old Gaelic and Brythonic literature which by then had taken its place in folklore. In the process, the mythologies, superstitions, beliefs and practices on which the literature drew were reinvented. New translations of ancient prose and poetry were offered to a Victorian society in a suitably honed and 'proper' language. Ireland has the oldest vernacular tradition of prose and poetry in Europe; emerging in the 6th century its energy has been sustained, unbroken, until the modern period. Prose, the vehicle for the heroic epics, is characterized by the kind of overstatement and absurdity that so well lends itself to satire. The poetry calls up the ancient beliefs of a vibrant nature religion that is by no means romantic; this is not the poetry of Wordsworth and Coleridge, drawing on an idealism or paradisiacal perception of nature in which humanity lives in perfect harmony with all created forms. Such rapture is certainly to be found, but it hides, timidly, behind Nature's more violent, unpredictable and omnipotent persona. Nature is mischievous, deadly, unremittingly perusing what, today, we understand is its genetically programmed progress towards secure survival. The poetry echoes the harshness of the gods of Nature's pantheon, whose whimsies and extravagances can only be addressed by human sacrifice. Expressive of humanity's response, the poetry evokes awe, astonishment and trepidation.

In Wales, the professionalism of the bardic tradition was maintained by a Guild of Bards who protected poetic form by means of a 'rule book' that required a nine-year apprenticeship and poems to be written for special occasions, and which offered a scale of payment measured by the length of time served. There were also professional storytellers, and the most enduring of the stories they told were put together between 1350 and 1410 CE in a collection known as the *Mabinogion*. Scottish texts, written in Brythonic, such as works attributed to Aneirin and Taliesin, go back to the 6th century; works in Gaelic include those of Dallan Forgaill, and in Latin, St Columba.

Celtic Christianity, which furnished some of the texts on which this collection draws, is also known as the Old British Church, and the Culdes Church. It was at first a distinctive and home-grown form of the religion, retaining much of its pagan, pre-Christian beliefs and lore. The Synod of Whitby, held in 664 CE, effected a crucial step in the Christianization of Britain begun in 597 CE by St Augustine. Tension existed between Celtic Christianity and that of England, which followed Rome, the variant practices running side by side. At the synod the Celtic King, Oswy, decided for St Peter and Rome and gradually Christianity in its Celtic form was subsumed by Catholicism. Inevitably, such pre-Christian mythologies that have survived have done so surreptitiously, through oral tradition gathered together and recorded in written form since the Middle Ages.

The Druids were a priestly class, widely spread through pre-Roman western Europe and Britain. The name 'Druid' may be derived from a word meaning oak, and there is an association with the mistletoe that was cut from it. A lack of primary sources makes it difficult to discern the Druid practices that were distinct from other forms of pagan animism, such as that of the pre-Christian Irish Celts. What seems clear is that Druids were custodians of ancient lore and wisdom, of astronomical and calendric knowledge, and given to prophecy, law-making and the almost holocaustic sacrifice of both animals and humans bound up in the huge wicker constructions described by Strabo and Caesar. Aspects of the lore survive in the celebration of Halloween, the making of corn-dollies and other harvest rituals, in the myths of Puck, woodwoses, the Green Man, and in superstitions loosely associated with luck and, specifically, with unlucky plants and animals.

In what sense can one speak of the 'sacredness' of these texts? Sacredness may take a very wide sweep of people, places and things. Priests, rabbis and lamas are thought to have acquired the attributes of sacredness, but so have seers, shamans and poets; synagogues, churches and mosques are assumed to be sacred places, but so maybe are wells, streams, groves or caves; the Hebrew Torah, the Guru Granth Sahib and the Eucharistic wine and bread are accepted as sacred things, so maybe are mistletoe, a staff cut from a hazel tree or a sheaf of corn; the imitation of Christ or the creation of a mandala is taken to be a sacred practice, so also is the veneration of an oak tree or a pupil's dialogue with his teacher. It is only in the reading and contemplation of these texts that their sacredness will become apparent. It will surprise many readers that heroic tales may be read not just as mythic history, but as parables of great spiritual enterprise, and of the courage and commitment needed to undertake it. It will surprise others that omens, cures, visions and anecdotes of animals and birds may be read as signs of the reverence due to everything, and of the miracle of the mundane.

Gerald Benedict

CREATION

THE CREATION STORY

An abbreviated version of the Genesis creation story, followed by an account of how the human race spread through and settled the then known world.

1. God made Heaven and Earth at the first, and He Himself hath no beginning nor ending.

2. He made first the formless mass, and the light of angels, on the first Sunday. He made firmament on the Monday. He made earth and seas on the Tuesday. He made sun and moon and the stars of Heaven on the Wednesday. He made birds of the air and reptiles of the sea on the Thursday. He made beasts of the earth in general, and Adam to rule over them, on the Friday. Thereafter God rested on the Saturday from the accomplishment of a new Creation, but by no means from its governance.

3. Thereafter, He gave the bailiffry of Heaven to Lucifer, with the nine orders of the Angels of Heaven. He gave the bailiffry of Earth to Adam and to Eve, with her progeny. Thereafter Lucifer sinned, so that he was leader of a third of the host of angels. The

King confined him with a third of the host of angels in his company, in Hell. And God said unto the Foe of Heaven: Haughty is this Lucifer, *unite et confundamus consilium eius.*

4. Thereafter Lucifer had envy against Adam, for he was assured that this would be given him Adam, the filling of Heaven in his Lucifer's room. Wherefore he Iofer Niger came in the form of the serpent, and persuaded Adam and Eve to sin, in the matter of eating of the apple from the forbidden tree. Wherefore Adam was expelled from Paradise into common earth.

5. Thereafter the Lord came to them, and He said unto Adam, 'of Earth you are and into earth you will go.' You will not obtain satisfaction without labour. He said further unto the woman, 'it shall be with insufferable pain that thou shalt bring forth thy sons'.

6. The progeny of Adam sinned thereafter, namely the elder of the sons of Adam, Cain the accursed, who slew his brother Abel … through his jealousy, and through his greed, with the bone of a camel, as

learned men say. In this manner began the kin-murders of the world.

7. As for Seth, one of the three sons of Adam who had progeny, of him are the men of the whole world. ... For it is Noe who is the second Adam, to whom the men of all the world are traced. For the Flood drowned the whole seed of Adam, except Noe with his three sons, Sem, Ham, Iafeth, and their four wives Coba, Olla, Oliva, Olivana. Afterwards, when God brought a Flood over the whole world, none of the people of the world escaped from the Flood except it be the people of that ark – Noe with his three sons, and the wife of Noe, the wives of his sons. ...

8. Now Sem settled in Asia, Ham in Africa, Iafeth in Europe.

Irish, 11th century (1)

THE CREATION OF THE ELEMENTS OF THE WORLD

'Concerning the creation of the elements of the world, and of man to reign over them naturally thereafter.'

V

'The Most High, foreseeing the mechanism and
   harmony of the world,
Had made heaven and earth, established sea and
   waters,
and the seeds of plants, and the bushes in thickets,
sun, moon, and stars, fir and all needful things,
birds, fish, and cattle, beasts and animals –
and last of all the first man, to rule them through
   foreknowledge.

VI

At the same time that the stars, the lights of the
   ether, were made,
the angels all praised the Lord, the Maker of
   heavenly things,
for his wondrous shaping of the enormous mass.

They proclaimed and exalted him without cease,
   as was fitting,
and gave thanks to God the Lord in splendid
   song –
out of love and free will, not simply from inborn
   nature.'

Scottish, 6th century (2)

THE BARDIC SECRET OF
THE ORIGINS AND PROGRESS
OF LETTERS AND THE NAME
OF GOD

Pray, my skilful and discreet teacher, if it be fair to ask, how was the knowledge of letters first obtained?

I will exhibit the information of men of wisdom and profound knowledge, thus: When God pronounced His name, with the word sprang the light and the life; for previously there was no life except God Himself. And the mode in which it was spoken was of God's direction. His name was pronounced, and with the utterance was the springing of light and vitality, and man, and every other living thing; that is to say, each and all sprang together. And Menw the Aged, son of Menwyd, beheld the springing of the light, and its form and appearance, not otherwise than thus, in three columns; and in the rays of light the vocalization – for one were the hearing and seeing, one unitedly the form and sound; and one unitedly with the form and sound was life, and one unitedly with these three was power, which power was God the Father. And since each of these was one unitedly, he understood that every voice, and hearing, and living, and being, and sight, and seeing, were one unitedly with God; nor is the least thing other than God. And by seeing the form, and in it hearing the voice, not otherwise, he knew what form and appearance voice should have. And having obtained earth under him co-instantaneously with the light, he drew the form of the voice and light on the earth. And it was on hearing the sound of the voice, which had in it the kind and utterance of three notes, that he obtained the three letters, and knew the sign that was suitable to one and other of them. Thus he made in form and sign the Name of God, after the semblance of rays of light, and perceived that they were the figure and form and sign of life; one also with them was life, and in life was God, that is to say, God is one with life, and there is no life but God, and there is no God but life.

It was from the understanding thus obtained in respect of this voice, that he was able to assimilate mutually every other voice as to kind, quality, and reason, and could make a letter suitable to the utterance of every sound and voice. Thus were obtained the Cymraeg [a member of the Brythonic branch of Celtic spoken natively in Wales] and every other language. And it was from the three primary letters that were constructed every other letter, which is the principal secret of the Bards of the Isle of Britain; and from this secret comes every knowledge of letters that is possible.

Welsh, 1862 (3)

THE EVERNEW TONGUE

The 'Evernew tongue' theme in Irish literature consists of dialogues between Hebrew sages gathered together on the summit of Mount Zion on the eve of Easter and the spirit of the apostle Philip. The term 'Evernew tongue' refers to the tradition that St Philip had his tongue cut out several times but it always grew again and he was able to continue preaching and teaching.

The wise men of the Hebrews asked, 'What existed at that time, when there existed none of the things which have so far been mentioned?'

The Evernew Tongue answered, 'There was That which was more wonderful than every creature: God without beginning, without end, without sorrow, without age, without decay. ... He thought something: that it would be nobler that his power and glory be seen – that which was inexpressible, that which existed in no other things though he existed himself.

In the same day he made the circuit of the shapes, that is, the material from which the world was made. For it is a round encircling shape which God first made as a shape for the world. ...'

'Though you do not see it,' he said, 'with respect to the shapes of the world, every creature has been established in roundness. For the seven heavens were established in a round circle, and the seven surrounding seas were made in a circle, and the lands were made in a circle, and it is in a round circle that the stars go around the round wheel of the world, and it is in roundness of form that souls are seen after parting from their bodies, and the circuit of the loft *riched* is seen to be round, and the shapes of the sun and moon are seen to be round. All that is fitting; for the Lord who has always been and who will always be, and who made all those things, is a circle without beginning, without end. That is why the world has been formed in a round shape.'

The Hebrews said, 'What was there in the many-shaped round circuit which was the material of the world?'

The Evernew Tongue answered, 'There were', he said, 'in the round circuit of the material of the world, cold and heat, light and darkness, heavy and light, liquid and dry, high and low, bitterness and mildness, strength and weakness, the roar of the sea and the crash of thunder, the scent of flowers and the chanting of angels and pillars of fire.'

Irish, 10th century (4)

LIFE

THE EARTHLY JOURNEY

Every journey has its stages, and for the purposes of these pages account is to be taken of the following:

1. Lustration, or lustral rites, whether by fire, by water, by milk or by blood.

2. Illumination, under which come premonitions, omens, divination, inclusive of second-sight. Here mysticism is recognized from the outset: it is so far a testimony to the fact that all human knowledge is in part.

3. Healing, passing in spiritual religion to salvation, wherein all healing culminates. It has its pre-shadowings in
   (a) The rites that unite. Here fall the ceremonies relating to espousals and marriage, and some forms of pagan eucharists.
   (b) The rites that avert. Here account is taken of the evil workings of envy; the effects of the evil eye; the belief that an issue of blood may be magically stopped; some phases of magic and of sacrifice.

(c) Faith-healing under psychic suggestion.
This is a constant element in human life, but it assumes lower and higher forms. Account is here taken of old elementary rites only, such as that at Loch Mo Nair; those at Holy Wells, such as Holywell; a special instance is the pilgrimage to Lough Derg (St Patrick's Purgatory).

Celtic, pre-Christian (5)

SO IS YOUR LIFE ...

As in the season of ice there are caught in the snares birds, seeking their food, and fish in nets, and none so much as dreamed till now of dying, yet now they are prepared for supper over the charcoal fire; so is your life, from beginning to end, which you pass in the world, always among sins, and if you do not amend them before the end of your days after all your pleasures, you will stay in the snare ...

Breton, 1519 (6)

ON DESTINY

The earthly body of man, his moral shell and spirit container, is moulded before birth by following a soul pattern drawn by destiny. Once born, many forces influence the life of man on Earth, but he is also given the responsibility of free choice. Notwithstanding this, the life of any man can only follow a course set by destiny, but while on that course, he can do as he wills.

Pre-Christian, 2nd century BCE–1st century CE (7)

ON WORK

There is a right way to labour, and there is a wrong way. There is also a way of labour that is full of song and a way that is silent; both play their part. Men should choose their form of labouring and not have it thrust upon them. In it, they should find contentment and self-expression, then it will not become wearisome.

The man who would be happy and content must seek a form of labour free from anxious thoughts and fanciful desires. It must bring satisfaction and confer benefit. These things have been said before, but I say them again: do not pursue vain hopes or seek too high a reward.

Ask only for a just return, and remain your own master.

'You can pray, "God helm me", when you have expended the last ounce of your strength, for he did not place man on Earth to play but to work. Duty, obligation and responsibility are the man makers, and these are slighted in the times and places where men are less than men. Always reach out beyond the frontiers of your limitations, for if you believe a thing to be impossible, then you yourself have made it so.'

Pre-Christian, 2nd century BCE–1st century CE (8)

ON MASTERING LIFE

Be a Master of Life; this is one who has his body and emotions firmly in reign. Though hard pressed by tribulations and afflictions, he remains steadfast; his mind is never confused. He knows what has to be done, what is expected of him, and does it. He strikes swiftly when action is needed, or just keeps plodding along the path. His mind is clear regarding his duty, and he knows his obligations and does not shirk them. He is always a pillar of strength to his weaker brethren.

Who are the Masters of Life? When you can ride the stormy seas of sorrow, when you are not overcome by pleasure, when you can control the passions, master fear, discard anger, and whatever comes, maintain a quiet and steady manner, you will be a Master of Life.

When you can accept all your obligations cheerfully, do your duty at all times, accept whatever comes, be it good or ill, with steadfast heart, remain calm in the midst of confusion and upheaval, you will be a Master of Life. When you can temper all your desires with prudence, resist temptations to weakness and bring all urges under control; when you can bring all senses into harmony, control all emotion, overcome the greed for possessions, smother unwholesome desires, you will be a Master of Life. When you can subdue anger, dispel dismay, never forget where your duty lies and be completely free from confusion of mind, you will be a Master of Life.

Pre-Christian, 2nd century BCE–1st century CE (9)

WELCOME ONE ANOTHER

Forget thy poverty for awhile;
Let us think of the world's hospitality
The Son of Mary will prosper thee
And every guest shall have his share.

Many a time
What is spent returns to the bounteous hand,
And that which is kept back
None the less has passed away.

Scottish, traditional (10)

RUNE OF HOSPITALITY

I saw a stranger yestreen:
I put food in the eating place,
Drink in the drinking place,
Music in the listening place:

And in the sacred name of the Trinity
He blessed myself and my house.
My cattle and my dear ones.
And the lark said in her song
    Often, often, often
Goes the Christ in the stranger's guise,
    Often, often, often
Goes the Christ in the stranger's guise.

Scottish, traditional (11)

PLACES

THE LAND OF IRELAND

'I invoke the land of Ireland
Shining, shining sea!
Fertile, fertile mountain!
Wooded vale!
Abundant river, abundant in waters!
Fish abounding lake!
Fish abounding sea!
Fertile earth!
Irruption of fish! Fish there!
Bird under wave! Great fish!
Crab hole! Irruption of fish!
Fish abounding sea!'
　　(Gildas ii. 4)

Irish, 1911 (12)

LAND OF MY FATHERS

The old land of my fathers is dear to me,
Land of poets and singers, famous men of renown;
Her brave warriors, very splendid patriots,
For freedom shed their blood.

Nation, Nation, I am true to my Nation.
While the sea is a wall to the pure, most loved
    land,
O may the old language endure.
Old mountainous Wales, paradise of the bard,

Every valley, every cliff, to me is beautiful.
Through patriotic feeling, so charming is the
    murmur
Of her brooks, rivers, to me.

If the enemy oppresses my land under his foot,
The old language of the Welsh is as alive as ever.
The muse is not hindered by the hideous hand of
    treason,
Nor is the melodious harp of my country.

Welsh, 1856 (13)

ELYSIUM

*The romantic beauty of Elysium is described in
these Celtic tales in a way unequalled in all
other sagas or Märchen, and it is insisted on
by those who come to lure mortals there. The
beauty of its landscapes – hills, white cliffs,
valleys, sea and shore, lakes and rivers – its
trees, inhabitants and birds – and the charm
of its summer haze, are obviously the product
of the imagination of a people keenly alive to
natural beauty. The opening lines sung by the
goddess to Bran strike a note which sounds
through all Celtic literature.*

'There is a distant isle, around which sea-horses
    glisten,
A beauty of a wondrous land, whose aspects are
    lovely,
Whose view is a fair country, incomparable in its haze.
It is a day of lasting weather, that showers silver
    on the land;
A pure white cliff on the range of the sea,
Which from the sun receives its heat.'

Welsh, traditional (14)

DEIRDRE LOOKED BACK ON THE LAND OF ALBA [SCOTLAND] AND SANG THIS LAY:

Beloved is that eastern land to me,
Alba with its lochs.
Oh that I might not depart from it,
Unless I were to go with Naos!
Beloved is the Forest Fort and high DunFin.
Beloved is the Dun above it.
Beloved is Innis Drayno
And beloved is Dun Sween.
The forest of the sea to which Ainnle would
    come, alas!

I leave for ever.
And Naos, on the seacoast of Alba.
Glen Lay, I would sleep by its gentle murmur.
Fish and venison, and the fat of meat boiled,
Such would be my food in Glen Lay.

Glenmassan! High is its wild garlic, fair its
    branches
I would sleep wakefully
Over the shaggy Invermasan.

Glen Etive! in which I raised my first house,
Delightful were its groves on rising
When the sun struck on Glen Etive.
My delight was Glen Orchy;
It is the straight vale of many ridges.
Joyful were his fellows around Naos
In Glen Urchay.

Glendaruadh
My delight in every man who belongs to it.
Sweet is the voice of the cuckoo
On the bending tree,
Sweet it is above Glendaruadh.
Beloved is Drayen of the sounding shore!
Beloved is Avich of the pure sand.
Oh that I might not leave the east
Unless it were to come along with me! Beloved

Scottish, 1238 (15)

IONA

Behold Iona!
A blessing on each eye that seeth it!
He who does a good for others
Here, will find his own redoubled
    Many-fold!

Scottish, 6th century (16)

MEN AND WOMEN

INITIATION INTO WOMANHOOD

In all, the initiate into womanhood learns responsibility, freedom, honour, and how to become a citizen of the clan. On the first day of her first mìosach (menstruation) she should take this charge:

'I vow as an honourable woman of my clan, to: Respect my woman's body with the care of a mother and the protection of a father. Honor my woman's mind with the challenge of strong thought and firm judgment. Empower my woman's spirit with the passion of truth and cultivation of love. All these things I vow in the names of the gods my clan swear by. If I am untrue to them, may the earth swallow me up, may the waters rush over my body, and may the sky come down on my head.'

Scottish/Irish, 6th century (17)

INITIATION INTO MANHOOD

'I vow …
Not to take life just for the sake of killing
Not to kill a beast lying down, or a bird sitting
Not to kill the mother of a brood, or an unfledged
    bird
Not to kill the mother of a suckling, or a suckling
    beast

'Not to sow seed just for the sake of sowing
Not to take advantage of a person whose wits are
    not about her
Not to sow seed on another's mother or wife, nor
    on a person who knows not the consequences.
Not to sow seed on the mother of a suckling babe,
    or a babe.'

Scottish/Irish, 6th century (18)

HANDFASTING

The term 'Handfasting' was once used in ancient Celtic ceremonies of betrothal and trial marriage, for a period of a year and a day.

'When we are handfasted, as we term it, we are man and wife for a year and a day; that space gone by, each may choose another mate, or, at their pleasure, may call the priest to marry them for life; and this we call handfasting.'

('The Monastery', Walter Scott)

INVOCATION

'We stand firmly here on the Land, the land that is our foundation, the land that is ever beneath us, the land that is our sure footing. We are surrounded by the Sea, the sea that nurtures and envelops us, the sea that is our eternal cloak. The Sky is above us, the sky who watches, the sky who protects us, the sky who is our endless guard. We are here in endless time and space, here in the Centre of the Three Realms, the centre of the Cosmos, the Centre of the ALL THERE IS.

'We are here in the midst of the Old Ones – the creative power of the cosmos, the binding energy of the universe, life force of ALL THAT IS. We stand centred with our feet on the ground of mother Earth out of whose depths comes the bounty that makes our lives possible. We stand with the sky above us – sheltering us, guarding us, holding sun and moon and skies and rainbows and clouds, all a part of the plan to keep us safe and secure. We stand surrounded by the water of life that is the sea and all the moisture that gives life to both our bodies and the earth herself – nurtured, rocked in peace by the waves on the beach or the tumbling falls. We stand in the midst of all that has been created, the beauty that has been given to us.

'And as we stand here, so surrounded and sheltered and held, we feel the love of the Divine Ones swirling around us. The very creative forces of the universe and the Gods that our people have sworn by from time out of mind are with us here to honour this occasion of the handfasting of their children. Ancestors of both the bride and groom are here with us to add their blessing and their strength and guidance for the road ahead.

The Spirits of this land that we have worked and loved and have come to call home are here to watch and to acknowledge and to bless and to remind us of our responsibility to the land. We honour the Gods and the Ancestors and the Spirits of the Land and all who are assembled as we witness the vows that our children have for each other.'

TO THE BRIDE AND GROOM

To the Groom by name

'When you became a man in the eyes of this people you vowed: (*as for Initiation into Manhood*)

'Are you now ready to take another vow to build a life with this woman, to build a household and your own hearth? This is not an easy task. There will be moments of great joy and moments of great passion, but there will also be moments when you are sure that the vision of liveliness you see before you today has been maniacally transformed into the most irritating, most annoying woman on the face of the planet. It is easy to hold to your commitment when there is joy or passion, but it is the vow you say today that will give your heart room to celebrate your love even in the midst of the most trying of times.'

The Groom to answer in the affirmative in his own words.

To the Bride by name

'When you became a woman of this people you vowed: (*as for Initiation into Womanhood*)

'Are you now ready to take a vow to build a life with this man, to become the heart of your own hearth? Tis not an easy task, my dear one. You will have moments when liquid love for you shines out of his eyes, and there will be moments that his touch excites you with fire, but there will also be times when you are sure that you are in the presence of the most exasperating, most opinionated, most irritating man in all the cosmos. It is in those times, that the words you say here today open your being to true compassion and absolute unconditional love.'

The Bride to answer in the affirmative in her own words.

'(*Name of groom*), are you willing to treasure this woman and honour her, protect her and joy in her? Are you willing to support her not only physically, but also emotionally and spiritually? (*If there are children involved you may add this*): Are you willing to be in the place of father/mother to her/his children and teach them and nourish them as if they were flesh of your flesh? (*Name of bride*), are you willing to treasure this man, honour and care for him and joy in him? Are you willing to support him not only physically, but also emotionally and spiritually? (*If there are children involved, you may add this*): Are you willing to share your children with him/her as you truly blend many into one? (*Names of children*), are you willing to be respectful to the Elders the Gods have gifted you with and be a part of this hearth? If you are so willing, now is the time to speak the words of the commitment you make to each other.'

The Bride and Groom, and children if they are present, speak the words they have for each other, and rings or other gifts can be exchanged.

THE BLESSINGS

(Specific blessings may be asked of patron saints, specific deities or other divine entities as specific to the people being married.)

'We ask the blessing of the Gods we swear by for these two people as they bind together these two Clans and their lives. We ask that in times of joy you would be present in their laughter, in times of trouble you would be their strength, in times of seeking you would be there to guide and in the changing times of human lives you would be the grounding and foundation that is unchanging. We honour you for your presence and your blessing.'

Bride's blessing (or insert blessing of other matron or saint)

'Bless this hearth Brid that your fire might kindle
our spirits and warm our hearts
Let our household echo laughter.
Filled with love where there was once hate
Joy where sadness dwelled
Warmth where we were once cold.
Guide us to peace
Lead us to love
And hold us close in your arms.
Hail to Brid, Lady of fire, burn bright here.'

Manannan's blessing (or blessing of other patron or saint)

'Manannan – we ask your blessing on this hearth
and these two so that when the waves come in
their lives, they might ride over them smoothly
even as your chariot rides over the waves of the
sea. When enemies seek to come against them,
defend them and keep them in the eye of the
storm. Let your treasures be blessings in their
lives of truth, strength, plenty and protection
from harm and the best of all blessings, that of
laughter. Manannan, let the sea that is our very

life blood, nurture this union and make this hearth strong.

'And of course, you have my blessing. May your hearts be filled with joy. May your hearth prosper. May your children grow into honourable men and women. May your compassion assuage your anger when it threatens to erupt. May your tolerance stay your tongue when it has sharpened itself into a cutting blade. May your patience with each other manifest in the spirit of compromise in the midst of differences. May you be strength for each other in times of weakness and ill health. May you be comfort for each other in times of sorrow. May the love you have for each other manifest as peace in your hearth.

'In the name of the Old Ones who have many names and many faces, known and unknown, In the name of the Gods our people have been swearing by from time immemorial, In the name of the One many of our people now swear by, in the presence of the ancestors, in the presence of the land spirits, in the presence of friends and family, I celebrate the love that is between you, I acknowledge the commitment made in your vows to each other, and I recognize your union.

'Three things a person gains when their mate endeavours to be excellent: their household peaceful for love of them, their children gentle in manners, and the respect of their neighbours.

'You may kiss the bride.'

Scottish, traditional (19)

BRIGIT HELPS THE MOTHER OF GOD

There was a poor man, and a poor woman, living in an ancient place in Ireland, a sort of a wilderness. The man used to be wishing for a son that would be a help to him with the work, but the woman used to say nothing, because she was good. They had a baby at last, but it was a girl, and the man was sorry and he said, 'We will always be poor now.' But the woman said, for it was showed to her at that time, 'This child will be the Mother of God.' The girl grew up in that ancient place, and one day she was sitting at the door, and our Saviour sent One to her that said 'Would you wish to be the Mother of God?' 'I would wish it' said she. And on the minute, as she said that, the Saviour went into her as a child. The Messenger took her with him then, and he put beautiful clothing on her, and she turned to be so beautiful that all the people followed them, crowding to see the two beautiful people that were passing by. They met then with Brigit, and the Mother of God said to her, 'What can we do to make these crowds leave following us?' 'I will do that for you' said Brigit 'for I will show them a greater wonder.' She went into a house then and brought out a harrow and held it up over her head, and every one of the pins gave out a flame like a candle; and all the people turned back to look at the shining harrow that was such a great wonder. And it is because of that the harrow is blessed since that time. The Mother of God asked her then what would she do for her as a reward. 'Put my day before your own day' said Brigit. So she did that, and Saint Brigit's day is kept before her own day ever since. And there are some say Brigit fostered the Holy Child, and kept an account of every drop of blood he lost through his lifetime, and anyway she was always going about with the Mother of God.

Irish, 7th century (20)

A POEM ABOUT EVE

I am Eve, great Adam's wife,
I that wrought my children's loss,
I that wronged Jesus of life,
By right 'tis I had borne the cross.

I a kingly house forsook,
Ill my choice and my disgrace,
Ill the counsel that I took,
Withering me and all my race.

I that brought the winter in
And the windy glistening sky,
I that brought terror and sin,
Hell and pain and sorrow.

Irish, 10th century (21)

CHARMS,
SUPERSTIONS
AND MAGIC

A TOOTHACHE CHARM

The incantation put by lovely Bride
Before the thumb of the Mother of God,
On lint, on wort, on hemp,
For worm, for venom, for teeth.

The worm that tortured me,
In the teeth of my head,
Hell hard by my teeth,
The teeth of hell distressing me.

The teeth of hell close to me;
As long as I myself shall last
May my teeth last in my head.

On lint, on comb, on agony.
On sea, on ocean, on coast.
On water, on lakes, on marshes.

THWARTING THE EVIL EYE

'The effects of the evil eye appear in yawning and
vomiting and in a general disturbance of the system.
The countenance assumes an appearance grim,
gruesome, and repulsive, "greann, greisne, and
grannda"'.

Who shall thwart the evil eye?
   I shall thwart it, methinks,
   In name of the King of life.
   Three seven commands so potent,
   Spake Christ in the door of the city;
   Pater Mary one,
   Pater King two,
   Pater Mary three,
   Pater King four,
   Pater Mary five,
   Pater King six,
   Pater Mary seven;
   Seven pater Maries will thwart
   The evil eye,
Whether it be on man or on beast,
   On horse or on cow;

Be thou in thy full health this night,
   [*The name*]
In name of the Father, the Son, and the Holy
   Spirit. Amen.

THE SHAMROCK OF LUCK

Thou shamrock of good omens,
Beneath the bank growing
Whereon stood the gracious Mary,
The Mother of God.

The seven joys are,
Without evil traces,
On thee, peerless one
Of the sunbeams –

Joy of health,
Joy of friends,
Joy of kine,
Joy of sheep,
Joy of sons, and
Daughters fair,
Joy of peace,
Joy of God!

The four leaves of the straight stem,
Five of the straight stem from the root of the
  hundred rootlets,
Thou shamrock of promise on Mary's Day,
Bounty and blessing thou art at all times.

GOD OF THE MOON

God of the moon, God of the sun,
God of the globe, God of the stars,
God of the waters, the land, and the skies,
Who ordained to us the King of promise.

It was Mary fair who went upon her knee,
It was the King of life who went upon her lap,
Darkness and tears were set behind,
And the star of guidance went up early.

Illumed the land, illumed the world,
Illumed doldrum and current,
Grief was laid and joy was raised,
Music was set up with harp and pedal-harp.

THE RED HAIR OF A WOMAN

The red hair of a woman,
The grey beard of a man,
Are love and luck to the sloven
Who gets them in the nest of the
    wheatear.

Early on the morning of Monday,
I heard the bleating of a lamb,

And the kid-like cry of snipe,
While gently sitting bent,

And the grey-blue cuckoo,
And no food on my stomach.

On the fair evening of Tuesday,
I saw on the smooth stone,
The snail slimy, pale,

And the ashy wheatear
On the top of the dyke of holes,
The foal of the old mare
Of sprauchly gait and its back to me.

And I knew from these
That the year would not go well with me.

OMEN OF THE SWANS

I heard the sweet voice of the swans,
At the parting of night and day,
Gurgling on the wings of travelling,
  Pouring forth their strength on high.

I quickly stood me, nor made I move,
A look which I gave from me forth
Who should be guiding in front?
  The queen of luck, the white swan.

This was on the evening of Friday,
My thoughts were of the Tuesday –
I lost my means and my kinsfolk
  A year from that Friday for ever.

Shoulds't thou see a swan on Friday,
In the joyous morning dawn,
There shall be increase on thy means and thy kin,
  Nor shall thy flocks be always dying.

OMEN OF THE CUCKOO

I heard the cuckoo with no food in my stomach,
I heard the stock-dove on the top of the tree,
I heard the sweet singer in the copse beyond,
And I heard the screech of the owl of the night.

I saw the lamb with his back to me,
I saw the snail on the bare flag-stone,
I saw the foal with his rump to me,
I saw the wheatear on a dyke of holes,
I saw the snipe while sitting bent,
And I foresaw that the year would not
    Go well with me.

Scottish, traditional (22)

ON CELTIC MAGIC

'Magic is one of the few things which it is important to
discuss at some length, were it only because, being the
most delusive of all the arts, it has everywhere and at
all times been most powerfully credited. Nor need it
surprise us that it has obtained so vast an influence, for
it has united in itself the three arts which have wielded

the most powerful sway over the spirit of man. Springing in the first instance from Medicine – a fact which no one can doubt – and under cover of a solicitude for our health, it has glided into the mind, and taken the form of another medicine, more holy and more profound. In the second place, bearing the most seductive and flattering promises, it has enlisted the motive of Religion, the subject on which, even at this day, mankind is most in the dark. To crown all it has had recourse to the art of Astrology; and every man is eager to know the future and convinced that this knowledge is most certainly to be obtained from the heavens. Thus, holding the minds of men enchained in this triple bond, it has extended its sway over many nations, and the Kings of Kings obey it in the East.'

Pliny, c77 CE (23)

KNOWLEDGE
AND WISDOM

FROM THE BARDIC TRIADS

(*Abred* = this world; *Gwynvyd* = the Upper World)

There are three primeval Unities, and more than one of each cannot exist: one God; one truth; and one point of liberty, and this is where all opposites are given equal weight.

Three things proceed from the three primeval Unities: all life; all goodness; all power.

God consists necessarily of three things: the greatest in respect of life; the greatest in respect of knowledge; and the greatest in respect of power; and there can only be one of what is greatest in any thing.

Three things it is impossible God should not be: whatever perfect goodness ought to be; whatever perfect goodness would desire to be; and whatever perfect goodness can be.

The three witnesses of God in respect of what He has done, and will do: infinite power; infinite knowledge; and infinite love; for there is nothing that these cannot perform, do not know, and will not bring to pass.

There are three primary contemporaries: man; liberty; and light.

The three necessary obligations of man: to suffer; to change; and to choose; and whilst he has the power of

choosing, the other two things are not known before
they happen.

The three equal elements of man: Abred and
Gwynvyd; necessity and liberty; evil and good; all are
given equal weight, man having the power of attaching
himself to the one he pleases.

From three things will the necessity of Abred fall on
man: from not endeavouring to obtain knowledge; from
non-attachment to good; and from attachment to evil;
occasioned by these things he will fall to his own kind
in Abred, whence he will return, as at first.

From three things will man fall of necessity in
Abred, though he has in everything else attached
himself to good: from pride even to Annwn; from
falsehood to a corresponding state of perception; and
from unmercifulness to a similarly disposed animal,
whence, as at first, he returns to humanity.

The three primaries of the state of man: the first
accumulations of knowledge, love, and power, without
death. This cannot take place, in virtue of liberty and
choice, previous to humanity: these are called the three
victories.

Three things has God given to every living being:
namely, the plenitude of his species; the distinction of
his individuality; and the characteristic of a primitive

spirit as different from another; this is what constitutes the complete self of every one as apart from another.

From understanding three things will ensue the diminution and subjugation of all evil and death: their nature; their cause; and their operation; and this will be obtained in Gwynvyd.

The three stabilities of knowledge: to have traversed every state of life; to remember every state and its incidents; and to be able to traverse every state, as one would wish, for the sake of experience and judgment; and this will be obtained in the circle of Gwynvyd.

There are three things on the wane: the dark; the false; and the dead.

Three things acquire strength daily, there being a majority of desires towards them: love; knowledge; and justice.

Welsh, c1560 (24)

A CELTIC COSMOGONY

In the beginning was the boundless Lir, an infinite depth, an invisible divinity, neither dark nor light, in whom were all things past and to be. There at the close of a divine day, time being ended, and the Nuts of Knowledge harvested, the gods partake of the Feast of

Age and drink from a secret fountain. Their being there is neither life nor death nor sleep nor dream, but all are wondrously wrought together. They lie in the bosom of Lir, cradled in the same peace, those who hereafter shall meet in love or war in hate. The Great Father and the Mother of the Gods mingle together and Heaven and Earth are lost, being one in the Infinite Lir.

Of Lir but little may be affirmed, and nothing can be revealed. In trance alone the seer might divine beyond his ultimate vision this being. It is a breath with many voices which cannot speak in one tone, but utters itself through multitudes. It is beyond the gods and if they were to reveal it, it could only be through their own departure and a return to the primeval silences. But in this is the root of existence from which springs the sacred Hazel whose branches are the gods: and as the mystic night trembles into dawn, its leaves and its blossoms and its starry fruit burgeon simultaneously and are shed over the waters of space.

We have first of all Lir, an infinite being, neither spirit nor energy nor substance, but rather the spiritual form of these, in which all the divine powers, raised above themselves, exist in a mystic union or trance. This is the night of the gods from which Mananan first awakens, the most spiritual divinity known to the ancient Gael, being the Gaelic equivalent of that Spirit which breathed on the face of the waters. He is the root of existence from which springs the Sacred Hazel, the symbol of life ramifying everywhere.

The love is changed into desire as it is drawn deeper into nature, and this desire builds up the Mid-world or World of the Waters. And, lastly, as it lays hold of the earthly symbol of its desire it becomes on Earth that passion which is spiritual death. … As this divinity emerges from its primordial state of ecstatic tenderness or joy in Lir, its divided rays, incarnate in form, enter upon a threefold life of spiritual love, of desire, and the dark shadow of love; and these three states have for themselves three worlds into which they have transformed the primal nature of Dana: a World of Immortal Youth: a Mid-world where everything changes with desire: and which is called from its fluctuations the World of the Waters: and lastly, the Earth-world where matter has assumed that solid form when it appears inanimate or dead.

Irish, 1918 (25)

THE COLLOQUY OF THE TWO SAGES

Conversations sometimes suggest a catechism, the content of which resonates with pre-Celtic Christianity, calling on ancient lore, metaphor and symbolism. Poetry emerges as the ultimate form of creation, with a creative energy of its own.

Ferchertne asked [Nede]

'A question my youth, from where have you come?'
'Not hard. The answer is –

> From the beam of a Sage.
> From his prudent wisdom,
> From his worthy perfection,
> From the splendour of sunrise,
> The hazel nuts of his poetic art,
> The circuits he follows,
> Man is measured by his excellence,
> By teaching the just law of truth,
> By ending falsehood,
> By making clear colours,
> By creating poetry.

You, my Master, where have you come from?'

Ferchertne answered,

'Not hard. The answer is, from —

> Beyond the columns of age,
> Beyond the streams of Galion,
> Beyond the seat of Nechtain's wife,
> Beyond the forearm of Nuada's wife,
> Beyond the land of the sun,
> Beyond the flowing of the moon,
> Beyond the umbilical cord of youth.'

'A question, my instructive young man, what is your name?'

Nede answered,

'Not hard. The answer is —

> Very small, very great,
> Very congenial, very firm.
> Anger of fire,
> Fire of oratory,
> Clamour for knowledge,
> Well of benefit,
> Sword of song,
> My skill in singing burns with fire.

And you, oh my senior, what is your spirit?'

Ferchertne answered,

'Not hard, the answer is –
>   Seer of wisdom,
>   Oratorical warrior, interrogator of small
>   statements,
>   Courting knowledge,
>   Weaving skill,
>   Repository of poetry,
>   Abundance of the sea,

A question, my young instructor, what poetry to you create?'

Nede answered,

'Not hard. The answer is –
>   Reddening a complexion,
>   Point of flesh,
>   Cleansing modesty,
>   Tossing away shamelessness,
>   Fostering poetic art,
>   Sheltering investigation,
>   Courting science,
>   Art from all mouths,
>   Scattering knowledge,
>   An island for speech,
>   A small court,

Herding poetic composition,
A place for the Elders,
Instructing couples,
(responding to) the kings request for stories ...

*And questioned again about his poetic genealogy, Nede
replied,*

'Not hard. The answer is –
    Son of poetry,
    Poetry son of study,
    Study son of discussion,
    Discussion son of great knowledge,
    Great knowledge son of inquiring,
    Inquiring son of great investigation,
    Investigation son of expert knowledge,
    Expert knowledge son of great interrogation,
    Great interrogation son of understanding,
    Understanding son of clarity,
    Clarity son of the three Goddesses of Poetry,

Irish, c1160 (26)

THE BOYHOOD OF FIONN

'Knowledge, may it be said, is higher than magic and is more to be sought. It is quite possible to see what is happening and yet not know what is forward, for while seeing is believing it does not follow that either seeing or believing is knowing. Many a person can see a thing and believe a thing and know just as little about it as the person who does neither. But Fionn would see and know, or he would understand a decent ratio of his visions. That he was versed in magic is true, for he was ever known as the Knowledgeable man. … It may be, too, that he know how events would turn, for he had eaten the Salmon of Knowledge.'

Irish, 12th century (27)

THE BECUMA OF THE WHITE SKIN

'There are good and evil people in this and in every other world, and the person who goes hence will go to the good or the evil that is native to him, while those who return come as surely to their due. … Under all wrong-doing lies personal vanity or the feeling that we are endowed and privileged beyond our fellows. … The mind flinches even from the control of natural law, and how much more from the despotism of its own separated likenesses, for if another can control me that other has usurped me, has become me, and how terribly I seem diminished by the seeming addition.

'This sense of separateness is vanity, and is the bed of all wrong-doing. For we are not freedom, we are control, and we must submit to our own function ere we can exercise it. Even unconsciously we accept the rights of others to all that we have, and if we will not share our good with them, it is because we cannot, having none; but we will yet give what we have, although that be evil. To insist on other people sharing in our personal torment is the first step towards insisting that they shall share our joy, as we shall insist when we get it.'

Irish, 12th century (28)

THE SALMON OF KNOWLEDGE

It is a story of a young man's adventures, I am relating for you this day. So as our hero followed the Boyne further and further upstream and into the mountains and glades of wild Ireland, the river became smaller and smaller until it resembled a stream. Finally he came to a well from which the stream poured. Nine old and purpled hazel trees encircled the well and it is said that there is a certain time when one of the trees will drop a hazelnut that, if caught by a salmon before it reaches the water, and said salmon is caught by a Druid before the fish gets back into the water, eating that salmon will bestow great wisdom and inspiration. Demne was not familiar with that tale, though his nose was familiar with the smell of fish over a fire.

Demne followed his nose a short distance away, passed by a couple of Oak trees, where he came to a clearing at the centre of which a fire was blazing and over the fire was a salmon cooking on a spit. There was no one to be seen, and the woods were quiet, as they often are when a stranger approaches. Demne cried out, 'Hello?' He heard no answer. He cried out again, a little louder 'Hello, is there anyone here?', still no answer. He cried out a third time in his booming voice, 'Hello, is anyone going to eat this here fish?' Demne was hungry, the fish smelled good and maybe the one that left it would not mind him tasting a wee bit.

So he reached down to taste a small piece of the salmon and in doing so he burned his thumb on the hot flesh. Immediately he stuck his thumb in his mouth to cool it. Just then he heard a soft voice, 'Hello, I see someone warming themselves by my fire.' Demne turned around to see a wise old Druid come into the clearing. They exchanged the warmest of courtesies as they did in the old days. The Druid asked Fionn if he tasted the fish. Demne, being an honourable man confessed he had. So the Druid, with a sigh, handed the fish over to the young man and said 'I suppose this is for you then.' Demne accepted the Druid's hospitality and while Demne was enjoying his meal, the wise man told Demne the story of the Salmon of Knowledge, and that the proper conditions to produce such a fish only happen but once every seven years. Demne, embarrassed by his hasty hunger, apologized for any inconvenience. The old Druid, smiling, explained that his patience will persevere for the next Salmon of Knowledge.

[The Druid renames him Fionn, for the glow of inspiration.]

Now, since Fionn's first taste of the fish was when he burnt his thumb upon it, whenever he found himself faced with a perplexing problem all he had to do was put his thumb in his mouth and think for a while. Soon the answer would come to him. This is how Fionn came onto the great knowledge he is said to have possessed. It served him well. Later he went on to be a King and the leader of an incredible band of exceptionally skilled

men, known as the fianna. I'll save that story for
another time.

Because of that knowledge Fionn became so famous
in his day, that it was said if ever a day went by that his
name was not mentioned, at least once – the world
would come to an end. So it is good fortune for the
world that I picked his story to tell and so goes the story
of Fionn MacCumhail and the Salmon of Knowledge.

Irish, 12th century (29)

A BARDIC PHILOSOPHY AND CATECHISM

THE PHILOSOPHY

There are two principles, or 'primary existences', God
and Cythrawl, who stand respectively for the principle
of energy tending towards life, and the principle of
destruction tending towards nothingness. *Cythrawl* is
the word used in the early literature for Hades [or
Fairyland] which may be rendered the Abyss, or Chaos.
In the beginning there was nothing but God and
Annwn. Organized life began by the Word – God
pronounced His ineffable Name and the 'Manred' was
formed. The Manred was the primal substance of the

universe. It was conceived as a multitude of minute indivisible particles – atoms, in fact – each being a microcosm, for God is complete in each of them, while at the same time each is a part of God, the Whole. The totality of being as it now exists is represented by three concentric circles. The innermost of them, where life sprang from Annwn, is called 'Abred', and is the stage of struggle and evolution – the contest of life with Cythrawl. The next is the circle of 'Gwynfyd', or Purity, in which life is manifested as a pure, rejoicing force, having attained its triumph over evil. The last and outermost circle is called 'Ceugant', or Infinity. Here all predicates fail us, and this circle, represented graphically not by a bounding line, but by divergent rays, is inhabited by God alone.

THE CATECHISM

Q. 'Whence didst thou proceed?'

A. 'I came from the Great World, having my beginning in Annwn.'

Q. 'Where art thou now? and how camest thou to what thou art?'

A. 'I am in the Little World, whither I came having traversed the circle of Abred, and now I am a Man, at its termination and extreme limits.'

Q. 'What wert thou before thou didst become a man, in the circle of Abred?'

A. 'I was in Annwn the least possible that was capable of life and the nearest possible to absolute death; and I came in every form and through every form capable of a body and life to the state of man along the circle of Abred, where my condition was severe and grievous during the age of ages, ever since I was parted in Annwn from the dead, by the gift of God, and His great generosity, and His unlimited and endless love.'

Q. 'Through how many different forms didst thou come, and what happened unto thee?'

A. 'Through every form capable of life, in water, in earth, in air. And there happened unto me every severity, every hardship, every evil, and every suffering, and but little was the goodness or Gwynfyd before I became a man. ... Gwynfyd cannot be obtained without seeing and knowing everything, but it is not possible to see or to know everything without suffering everything. ... And there can be no full and perfect love that does not produce those things which are necessary to lead to the knowledge that causes Gwynfyd.'

Every being, we are told, shall attain to the circle of Gwynfyd at last.

Irish/Scottish, traditional (30)

ON FREE WILL

Go your own ways; follow your undisturbing beliefs. Had it been in accord with the Creating Intent, you could all have been more perfect in righteousness, but what would you have been then? Mere puppets dangling from the hand above. The Divine intent was not to create puppets; what end could they serve? The Supreme Spirit wants men, men with freewill capable of decision, free men reaching upwards to divinity, choosing it of their own accord.

Pre-Christian, 2nd century BCE–1st century CE (31)

THE DRUID AND THE CHILD

Druid: Calm now, beautiful child of the Druid; answer, what would you have me sing you?

Child: Sing the number twelve to me, until I've learned it today.

Druid: Twelve months and twelve signs; the last but one, the Sagittarius lets fly his arrow armed with a point.

The twelve signs are at war. The beautiful Cow; the black Cow bearing a white star on her forehead comes out of the forest of Mortal Remains;

In her chest is the sting of the arrow; she's bleeding profusely, she is growning, head lifted:

The horn is heard; fire and thunder, rain and wind, thunder and fire, nothing, no more, nor any series!

Eleven Priests armed, from Vannes, with their swords broken; And their bloody robes and crutches of hazel wood; three hundred more than they are, eleven of them.

Ten enemy ships have been seen coming from Nantes: woe betides you! Woe betide you! Men of Vannes.

Nine white little hands on the table in the open air, near the tower of Lerzarmeur, and nine mothers who moan a lot.

Nine dwarfs dancing around the fountain, with flowers in their hair and dresses of white wool, in the light of the full moon.

The sow and her nine young wild boars, at the door of their lair, groaning and burrowing, burrowing and groaning; come! come! come! Hurry back to the apple tree! The old boar will give you a lesson.

Eight winds blowing; eight fires with the Great Fire lit in May on the mountain of war. Eight heifers white as foam, which graze the grass of the island deep; the eight white heifers of the Lady.

Seven suns and seven moons, seven planets, including the Hen. Seven elements including the flour of the air (the atoms).

Six small children of wax, enlivened by the energy of the moon, if you ignore it, I know it.

Six medicinal plants in the small pot; the small dwarf mixes the beverage, his little finger in his mouth.

Five parts of the land: five age groups in the length of time, five rocks on our sister.

Four sharpening stones, the sharpening stones belonging to Merlin, which hone the swords of the brave.

Three: There are three parts in the world: three beginnings and three purposes for the man as for the oak. Three kingdoms of Merlin, full of golden fruit, full of brilliant flowers, full of small children's laughter.

Two oxen yoked together; they pull, they will expire; see the wonder!

One. No series for the number *one*: the single Need, the Death, the father of Pain; nothing before, nothing more.

Breton, traditional (32)

CONFESSIONS, PRAYERS AND INVOCATIONS

THE CONFESSION OF
ST PATRICK

I, Patrick, a sinner, a most simple countryman, the least of all the faithful and most contemptible to many, had for father the deacon Calpurnius, son of the late Potitus, a priest, of the settlement of Bannavem Taburniae; he had a small villa nearby where I was taken captive. I was at that time about sixteen years of age. I did not, indeed, know the true God; and I was taken into captivity in Ireland with many thousands of people, according to our deserts, for quite drawn away from God, we did not keep his precepts, nor were we obedient to our priests who used to remind us of our salvation. And the Lord brought down on us the fury of his being and scattered us among many nations, even to the ends of the earth, where I, in my smallness, am now to be found among foreigners.

And there the Lord opened my mind to an awareness of my unbelief, in order that, even so late, I might remember my transgressions and turn with all my heart to the Lord my God, who had regard for my insignificance and pitied my youth and ignorance. And he watched over me before I knew him, and before I learned sense or even distinguished between good and evil, and he protected me, and consoled me as a father would his son. Therefore, indeed, I cannot keep silent, nor would it be proper, so many favours and graces have the Lord deigned to bestow on me in the land of my captivity. For after chastisement from God, and recognizing him, our way to repay him is to exalt him and confess his wonders before every nation under heaven. For there is no other God, nor ever was before, nor shall be hereafter.

Irish, c450 CE (33)

THE CLEARING FROM GUILT

To prove innocence of a crime a certain ancient form is gone through, which the people look on with great awe, and call it emphatically 'The Clearing'. It is a fearful ordeal, and instances are known of men who have died of fear and trembling from having passed through the terrors of the trial, even if innocent. And it is equally terrible for the accuser as well as the accused.

On a certain day fixed for the ordeal the accused goes to the churchyard and carries away a skull. Then, wrapped in a white sheet, and bearing the skull in his hand, he proceeds to the house of the accuser, where a great crowd has assembled; for the news of 'A Clearing' spreads like wildfire, and all the people gather together as witnesses of the ceremony. There, before the house of his accuser, he kneels down on his bare knees, makes the sign of the cross on his face, kisses the skull, and prays for some time in silence; the people also wait in silence, filled with awe and dread, not knowing what the result may be. Then the accuser, pale and trembling, comes forward and stands beside the kneeling man; and with uplifted hand adjures him to speak the truth. On which the accused, still kneeling and holding the skull in his hand, utters the most fearful imprecation known in the Irish language; almost as terrible as that curse of the Druids, which is so awful that it never yet was put into English words. The accused prays that if he fail to speak the truth all the sins of the man whose skull he holds may be laid upon his soul, and all the sins of his forefathers back to Adam, and all the punishment due to them for the evil of their lives, and all their weakness and sorrow both of body and soul be laid on him both in this life and in the life to come for evermore. But if the accuser has accused falsely and out of malice, then may all the evil rest on his head through this life for ever, and may his soul perish everlastingly.

It would be impossible to describe adequately the awe with which the assembled people listen to these terrible words, and the dreadful silence of the crowd as they wait to see the result. If nothing happens the man rises from his knees after an interval, and is pronounced innocent by the judgment of the people, and no word is ever again uttered against him, nor is he shunned or slighted by the neighbours. But the accuser is looked on with fear and dislike, he is considered unlucky, and seeing that his life is often made so miserable by the coldness and suspicion of the people, many would rather suffer wrong than force the accused person to undergo so terrible a trial as 'The Clearing'.

Irish, traditional (34)

CONSCIENCE

'Conscience is the eye of God in man, and the prudent man lets nothing be seen which is unworthy, unwholesome or unmanly. He is always circumspect in speech, for only those who can unring a bell are able to recall words spoken in haste. If Earth were devoid of evil, how could we know what was good and judge the weak from the strong? How would we know what to strive against the progress?'

Pre-Christian, 2nd century BCE–1st century CE (35)

RUNE BEFORE PRAYER

I am bending my knee
In the eye of the Father who created me,
In the eye of the Son who purchased me,
In the eye of the Spirit who cleansed me,
    In friendship and affection.
Through Thine own Anointed One, O God,
Bestow upon us fullness in our need,
    Love towards God,
    The affection of God,
    The smile of God,
    The wisdom of God,
    The grace of God,
    The fear of God,
    And the will of God
To do on the world of the Three,
As angels and saints
Do in heaven;
    Each shade and light,
    Each day and night,
    Each time in kindness,
    Give Thou us Thy Spirit.

Scottish, traditional (36)

[89]

FRAGMENT

As it was,
As it is,
As it shall be
Evermore,
O Thou Triune
Of grace!
With the ebb,
With the flow,
O Thou Triune
Of grace!
With the ebb,
With the flow.

Scottish, n.d. (37)

GOD WITH ME

God with me lying down,
God with me rising up,
God within in each ray of light,
Nor I a ray of joy without Him,
    Nor one ray without Him.

Christ with me sleeping,
Christ with me waking,
Christ with me watching,
Every day and night,
    Each day and night.

God with me protecting,
The Lord with me directing,
The Spirit with me strengthening,
For ever and for evermore,
    Ever and evermore, Amen.
        Chief of chiefs, Amen.

Scottish, traditional (38)

THE INVOCATION OF THE GRACES

I bathe thy palms
In showers of wine,
In the lustral fire,
In the seven elements,
In the juice of the rasps,
In the milk of honey,
And I place the nine pure choice graces

In thy fair fond face,
The grace of form,
The grace of voice,
The grace of fortune,
The grace of goodness,
The grace of wisdom,
The grace of charity,

The grace of choice maidenliness,
The grace of whole-souled loveliness,
The grace of goodly speech.

Dark is yonder town,
Dark are those therein,
Thou art the brown swan,
Going in among them.
Their hearts are under thy control,
Their tongues are beneath thy sole,
Nor will they ever utter a word
To give thee offence.

A shade art thou in the heat,
A shelter art thou in the cold,
Eyes art thou to the blind,
A staff art thou to the pilgrim,

An island art thou at sea,
A fortress art thou on land,
A well art thou in the desert,
 Health art thou to the ailing.

Thine is the skill of the Fairy Woman,
Thine is the virtue of Bride the calm,
Thine is the faith of Mary the mild,
Thine is the tact of the woman of Greece,
Thine is the beauty of Emir the lovely,
Thine is the tenderness of Darthula delightful,
Thine is the courage of Maebh the strong,
Thine is the charm of Binne-bheul.

Thou art the joy of all joyous things,
Thou art the light of the beam of the sun,
Thou art the door of the chief of hospitality,
Thou art the surpassing star of guidance,
Thou art the step of the deer of the hill,
Thou art the step of the steed of the plain,
Thou art the grace of the swan of swimming,
 Thou art the loveliness of all lovely desires.

The lovely likeness of the Lord
Is in thy pure face,
The loveliest likeness that
Was upon earth.

The best hour of the day be thine,
The best day of the week be thine,
The best week of the year be thine,
The best year in the Son of God's domain be thine.

Peter has come and Paul has come,
James has come and John has come,
Muriel and Mary Virgin have come,
Uriel the all-beneficent has come,
Ariel the beauteousness of the young has come,
Gabriel the seer of the Virgin has come,
Raphael the prince of the valiant has come,
And Michael the chief of the hosts has come,
And Jesus Christ the mild has come,
And the Spirit of true guidance has come,
And the King of kings has come on the helm,
To bestow on thee their affection and their love,
To bestow on thee their affection and their love.

Scottish, traditional (39)

BROCCAN'S HYMN TO SAINT BRIGIT

Victorious Brigit did not love the world:
she perched in it like bird on a cliff.
The Saint slept like a prisoner,
longing for her Son.

Not much fault was found with her
with regard to lofty faith in the Trinity.
Brigit, mother of my Over-King,
was born as the best in the kingdom of heaven.

She was not slanderous, she was not mischievous
she was not a lover of vehement women's quarrels,
she was not a stinging speckled snake,
she did not sell God's Son for grain.

She was not greedy for treasures;
she gave without resentment, without stint.
She was not hard or stingy,
she did not love to enjoy the world's goods.

She was not harsh towards guests;
she was kind to the unfortunate in their sickness.

She built an enclosure in the plain:
may it keep us, in our multitudes, safe for the
    Kingdom!
She did not tend her herd in the uplands,
but did her works in the midst of a plain.
She was a marvellous ladder whereby the tribes
could reach the kingdom of the Son of Mary.

Wondrous was Brigit's company,
wondrous the region to which she ascended.
She can meet with Christ alone,
something which is usual for assemblies.

Irish, 5th century (40)

THE DEER'S CRY

*This prayer of St Patrick's, composed in
433 CE, is also known as 'The Breastplate of
St Patrick' and 'The Lorica'. Having been told
that the Druids had laid an ambush to kill
him, St Patrick and his group offered this
prayer as they travelled to the King's court.
When the party drew near, all the Druids saw
was a doe and twenty fawns.*

I arise today through a mighty strength, the invocation of the Trinity, through belief in the Threeness, through confession of the Oneness of the Creator of creation.

I arise today through the strength of Christ with his Baptism, through the strength of His Crucifixion with His Burial, through the strength of His Resurrection with His Ascension, through the strength of His descent for the Judgment of Doom.

I arise today through the strength of the love of Cherubim in obedience of Angels, in the service of the Archangels, in hope of resurrection to meet with reward, in prayers of Patriarchs, in predictions of Prophets, in preachings of Apostles, in faiths of Confessors, in innocence of Holy Virgins, in deeds of righteous men.

I arise today, through the strength of Heaven; light of Sun, brilliance of Moon, splendour of Fire, speed of Lightning, swiftness of Wind, depth of Sea, stability of Earth, firmness of Rock.

I arise today, through God's strength to pilot me: God's might to uphold me, God's wisdom to guide me, God's eye to look before me, God's ear to hear me, God's word to speak for me, God's hand to guard me, God's way to lie before me, God's shield to protect me, God's host to secure me: against snares of devils, against temptations of vices, against inclinations of nature, against everyone who shall wish me ill, afar and anear, alone and in a crowd.

I summon today all these powers between me (and these evils): against every cruel and merciless power that may oppose my body and my soul, against incantations of false prophets, against black laws of heathenry, against false laws of heretics, against craft of idolatry, against spells of witches, smiths and wizards, against every knowledge that endangers man's body and soul. Christ to protect me today against poisoning, against burning, against drowning, against wounding, so that there may come abundance in reward.

Christ with me, Christ before me, Christ behind me, Christ in me, Christ beneath me, Christ above me, Christ on my right, Christ on my left, Christ in breadth, Christ in length, Christ in height, Christ in the heart of every man who thinks of me, Christ in the mouth of every man who speaks of me, Christ in every eye that sees me, Christ in every ear that hears me.

I arise today through a mighty strength, the invocation of the Trinity, through belief in the Threeness, through confession of the Oneness of the Creator of creation. Salvation is of the Lord. Salvation is of the Lord. Salvation is of Christ. May Thy Salvation, O Lord, be ever with us. Amen.

Irish, 433 CE (41)

DESIRES

May I speak each day according to Thy justice,
Each day may I show Thy chastening, O God;
May I speak each day according to Thy wisdom,
Each day and night may I be at peace with Thee.

Each day may I count the causes of Thy mercy,
May I each day give heed to Thy laws;
Each day may I compose to Thee a song,
May I harp each day Thy praise, O God.

May I each day give love to Thee, Jesu,
Each night may I do the same;
Each day and night, dark and light,
May I laud Thy goodness to me, O God.

Scottish, traditional (42)

THE NEW MOON

*This prayer is said by old men and women in
the islands of Barra. The fragment of moon-
worship is now a matter of custom rather than
of belief, although it exists over the whole of
the British Isles. It is a Christianized remnant
of a far more ancient religion.*

In name of the Holy Spirit of grace,
In name of the Father of the City of peace,
In name of Jesus who took death off us,
Oh! in name of the Three who shield us in every
    need,
If well thou hast found us to-night,
Seven times better mayest thou leave us without
    harm,
      Thou bright white Moon of the seasons,
      Bright white Moon of the seasons.

Scottish, traditional (43)

INVOCATION

The tongue of Columba in my head,
The eloquence of Columba in my speech.
The composure of the Victorious Son of grace
    Be mine in presence of the multitude.

Scottish, traditional (44)

THE
SPIRITUAL
LIFE

RESPECTING RELIGION

'Three foundations of Spirituality:
Hearth as altar,
work as worship,
service as sacrament.'

Celtic, pre-Christian (45)

RESPECTING THE TRUE HUMAN

'The three highest causes of the true human are:
Truth,
Honour and
Duty.

The three manifestations of the true human are:
Civility,
Generosity and
Compassion.'

Celtic, pre-Christian (46)

THE IMPRESS OF GOOD
AND EVIL

'Every thought leaves an impress upon the Spirit of
the Shadow self for good or evil. With every impress
of evil, there is further corruption and distortion of the
Spirit Form. With every impress of good, there is a
strengthening force, which beautifies the Spirit Form,
and so it resides within in joy and content.'

Celtic, pre-Christian (46)

THE SOUL

The Soul is supreme above all. It should be master of its
own forces and never permit itself to be led by its
servants – the senses. The purpose of the moral
restrictions and discipline imposed by religion is to
give it mastery, even as bodily discipline and proper
care result in a healthful physical existence.

The Soul is awakened by love, by happiness and
sorrow. The Soul acts upon the body, but the body does
not act upon the soul, for mind commands matter. The
Soul, awakening to conscious realization, becomes one
with the law and is no longer the slave of external

conditions but the heir to truth. It is capable of rising above the illusions and uncertainties inherent in matter.

Pre-Christian, 2nd century BCE–1st century CE (48)

THE BLAMELESSNESS OF THE SOUL

Soul, since I was made in necessity blameless
True it is, woe is me that thou shoulds't have come
    to my design,
Neither for my own sake, nor for death, nor for
    end, nor for beginning.
It was with seven faculties that I was thus blessed,
With seven created beings I was placed for
    purification;
I was gleaming fire when I was caused to exist;
I was dust of the earth, and grief could not reach
    me;
I was a high wind, being less evil than good;
I was a mist on a mountain seeking supplies of
    stags;
I was blossoms of trees on the face of the earth.

If the Lord had blessed me, He would have placed
   me on matter.
Soul, since I was made –

Welsh, c1250 (49)

COMPASSION AND CONSCIENCE

'Have a warm and compassionate heart. As frozen water
cannot cleanse the body, neither can a frozen heart
wash impure stains from the soul. The knightly man
treasures nothing so much as his honour, which marks
him as a man of high estate. Honour may be an attribute
of the poor man, for it is not dependent on riches or
station.'

Pre-Christian, 2nd century BCE–1st century CE (50)

THE RULE OF CORMAC MAC CULENDÁIN

1. Lasting, low-voiced congregation, happy the hour if
   I could learn it. The high knowledge feeds me, the
   melodius song of the believers.

2. Let us sing the song which the ancients have sung, the course which they have sounded forth. Would that I could expel from my flesh what they have expelled.

3. A grateful gift is speech without boasting, to be ever at the will of the King. Humility to fitting folk would be no folly, no disadvantage.

4. Due celebration, with patience, it is the ornament of every great work, we praise it. Silence when it is necessary. Eyelids towards heaven …

5. Stepping with dignity past kings. Renunciation of wine and flesh. Pure choice of a fair glorious grade, a humble, learned confessor.

6. Order of confession; perpetual sorrow; walking with knowledge; little sound. Rule fair-wondrous, pure; not to be at hateful lying.

7. 'Tis no evil heresy, 'tis no peradventure: God's love demands His fear. A walking without wicked pride from the Devil; not to be one hour in arrogance.

8. Patience, purity, with holiness; a putting away of hypocrisy with perversity. A holy dinner without repletion, without a full meal; a small fair ration; being a-fasting.

9. Fasting when it is proper; the excellent restraint which it brings. Solution of questions in time of faith deserves that there come not heresy.

10. A load of devotion with gentleness, pure, without sorrow. The mind towards bright eternal heaven. The selling of darkness for light.

11. An emaciated, miserable body. Study with a well-spoken old man. Intentness on conversing with the Canon. Forgetfulness of the wretched paltry world.

12. A protection of the soul, an approach to heaven, a wonderful power, a fostering of purity, is the food which is after extinction of desire, Christ's body with the blood of Mary's Son.

13. White raiment after the fashion of an elder, soul food ... I deem enough for my King at the completion of earthly life.

14. Let it be a deed of wisdom without danger. Let us escape from folly, from destruction …

Irish, 9th century (51)

THE RELIGION OF THE ANCIENT DRUIDS

'As one of their leading dogmas they inculcate this: that souls are not annihilated, but pass after death from one body to another, and they hold that by this teaching men are much encouraged to valour, through disregarding the fear of death. They also discuss and impart to the young many things concerning the heavenly bodies and their movements, the size of the world and of our earth, natural science, and of the influence and power of the immortal gods.'

'The whole Gaulish nation is to a great degree devoted to superstitious rites; and on this account those who are afflicted with severe diseases, or who are engaged in battles and dangers, either sacrifice human beings for victims, or vow that they will immolate themselves, and these employ the Druids as ministers for such sacrifices, because they think that, unless the life of man be repaid for the life of man, the will of the immortal gods cannot be appeased. They also ordain national offerings of the same kind. Others make wicker-work images of vast size, the limbs of which they fill with living men and set on fire.'

Caesar on the Druids (52)

POETIC RECORD OF SACRIFICE TO THE PAGAN GOD

'Here used to be
A high idol with many fights,
Which was named the Cromm Cruaich;
It made every tribe to be without peace.

''T was a sad evil!
Brave Gaels used to worship it.
From it they would not without tribute ask
To be satisfied as to their portion of the hard world.

'He was their god,
The withered Cromm with many mists,
The people whom he shook over every host,
The everlasting kingdom they shall not have.

'To him without glory
They would kill their piteous, wretched offspring
With much wailing and peril,
To pour their blood around Cromm Cruaich.

'Milk and corn
They would ask from him speedily
In return for one-third of their healthy issue:
Great was the horror and the scare of him.

'To him
Gaels would prostrate themselves,
From the worship of him, with many manslaughters,
The plain is called 'Mag Slecht".

'They did evil,
They beat their palms, they pounded their bodies,
Wailing to the demon who enslaved them,
They shed falling showers of tears.

'Around Cromm Cruaich
There the hosts would prostrate themselves;
Though he put them under deadly disgrace,
Their name clings to the noble plain.

'In their ranks stood
Four times three stone idols;
To bitterly beguile the hosts,
The figure of the Cromm was made of gold.

'Since the rule
Of Herimon, the noble man of grace,
There was worshipping of stones
Until the coming of good Patrick of Macha.

'A sledge-hammer to the Cromm
He applied from crown to sole,
He destroyed without lack of valour
The feeble idol which was there.'

Irish, c1160 (53)

ON PEACE OF MIND

If someone wrongs you without cause, do not let this
disturb your tranquillity of mind. Do nothing else
except scorn them. In this way, you will not be
unnecessarily upset, but will also be revenged without
any need for inflicting it. The tearing wind and flashing
darts of lightning leave the sun and moon untroubled;
their anger is vented on trees and plants below. So it is

with wrongs done by mortals; the wrongs do not disturb the hearts of superior men, but cause turmoil in the fainter hearts of inferior men.

Pre-Christian, 2nd century BCE–1st century CE (54)

ON TRUTH, AND THINGS AS THEY REALLY ARE

Things as you see them, and things as they really are, are in no way alike; illusion is the environment of Earth and it deludes the inner eye with outward impressions. As a needle pricks a blister to let out the water, so does the sharp point of Truth pierce the veil of illusion and let out ignorance.

The mind of man is like a pool of water; while it is disturbed, only distorted pictures can be seen; but when it becomes calm and still, the light of spiritual Truth is reflected there in all its beauty. The inner being interprets things through a veil of emotion. The man who burns hotly within himself sees the world about him as a fierce fire seeking to consume him; but the man who is calm and quiet within himself sees all about him as tranquil and peaceful.

Pre-Christian, 2nd century BCE–1st century CE (55)

ON WORSHIP

There is much talk among you concerning the nature of worship. Understand this: true worship is seeking to unite the spirit below with the Spirit Above. To do this you must have a heart purged of evil thoughts, a tongue undefiled by falsehood or tainted with deceit and hypocrisy, and a life free of all malice and hatred. Even this is not good enough; you must have a life filled with love and good deeds. Only when in this state are you fit to worship.

Pre-Christian, 2nd century BCE–1st century CE (56)

VISIONS AND
MYSTICISM

THE WORLD OF FAERY

'There is a difference between this world and the world of Faery, but it is not immediately perceptible. Everything that is here is there, but the things that are there are better than those that are here. All things that are bright are there brighter. There is more gold in the sun and more silver in the moon of that land. There is more scent in the flowers, more savour in the fruit. There is more comeliness in the men and more tenderness in the women. Everything in Faery is better by this one wonderful degree, and it is by this betterness you will know that you are there if you should every happen to get there.'

Irish, traditional (57)

THE THREE CAULDRONS OF POESY

My perfect cauldron of warming
has been taken by the Gods from the mysterious
    abyss of the elements;
a perfect truth that ennobles from the centre of
    being,

that pours forth a terrifying stream of speech.
I am Amergin White-knee,
with pale substance and grey hair,
accomplishing my poetic incubation in proper
    forms,
in diverse colours.
The Gods do not give the same wisdom to
    everyone,
tipped, inverted, right-side-up;
no knowledge, half-knowledge, full knowledge –
for Eber Donn, the making of fearful poetry,
of vast, mighty draughts, death-spells, of great
    chanting;
in active voice, in passive silence, in the neutral
    balance between,
in rhythm and form and rhyme,
in this way is spoken the path and function of my
    cauldrons.

Where is the root of poetry in a person; in the body or
in the soul? Some say it is in the soul, for the body does
nothing without the soul. Some say it is in the body
were the arts are learned, passed through the bodies of
our ancestors. It is said that this is the truth remaining
over the root of poetry, and the wisdom in every

person's ancestry does not come from the northern sky into everyone, but into every other person.

What then is the root of poetry and every other wisdom? Not hard; three cauldrons are born in every person – the cauldron of warming, the cauldron of motion and the cauldron of wisdom.

The cauldron of warming is born upright in people from the beginning. It distributes wisdom to people in their youth.

The cauldron of motion, however, increases after turning; that is to say it is born tipped on its side, growing within.

The cauldron of wisdom is born on its lips and distributes wisdom in poetry and every other art.

The cauldron of motion then, in all artless people is on its lips. It is side-slanting in people of bardcraft and small poetic talent. It is upright in the greatest of poets, who are great streams of wisdom. Not every poet has it on its back, for the cauldron of motion must be turned by sorrow or joy.

Question: How many divisions of sorrow turn the cauldrons of sages? Not hard; four: longing and grief, the sorrows of jealousy, and the discipline of pilgrimage to holy places. These four are endured internally, turning the cauldrons, although the cause is from outside.

There are two divisions of joy that turn the cauldron of wisdom; divine joy and human joy.

There are four divisions of human joy among the wise – sexual intimacy, the joy of health and prosperity after the difficult years of studying poetry, the joy of wisdom after the harmonious creation of poems, and the joy of ecstasy from eating the fair nuts of the nine hazels of the Well of Segais in the Sidhe realm. They cast themselves in multitudes, like a ram's fleece upon the ridges of the Boyne, moving upstream swifter than racehorses driven on midsummer's day every seven years.

The Gods touch people through divine and human joys so that they are able to speak prophetic poems and dispense wisdom and perform miracles, giving wise judgment with precedents, and blessings in answer to every wish. The source of these joys is outside the

person and added to their cauldrons to cause them to
turn, although the cause of the joy is internal.

    I sing of the cauldron of wisdom
    which bestows the nature of every art,
    through which treasure increases,
    which magnifies every artisan,
    which builds up a person through their gift.

    I sing of the cauldron of motion
    understanding grace,
    accumulating wisdom
    streaming ecstasy as milk from the breast,
    it is the tide-water of knowledge
    union of sages
    stream of splendour
    glory of the lowly
    mastery of speech
    swift intelligence
    reddening satire
    craftsman of histories
    cherishing pupils
    looking after binding principles
    distinguishing meanings
    moving toward music

propagation of wisdom
enriching nobility
ennobling the commonplace
refreshing souls
relating praises
through the working of law
comparing of ranks
pure weighing of nobility
with fair words of the wise
with streams of sages,
the noble brew in which is boiled
the true root of all knowledge
which bestows according to harmonious principle
which is climbed after diligence
which ecstasy sets in motion
which joy turns
which is revealed through sorrow;
it is enduring fire
undiminishing protection.
I sing of the cauldron of motion.

The cauldron of motion
bestows, is bestowed
extends, is extended
nourishes, is nourished

magnifies, is magnified
invokes, is invoked
sings, is sung
keeps, is kept,
arranges, is arranged,
supports, is supported.

Good is the well of poetry,
good is the dwelling of speech,
good is the union of power and mastery
which establishes strength.

It is greater than every domain,
it is better than every inheritance,
it bears one to knowledge,
adventuring away from ignorance.

Irish, traditional (58)

TUAN MAC CARILL TELLS HIS STORY

The memories of ancestors pass through several reincarnations which in the tradition of Celtic shamanism can take the form of different animals, until rebirth as a human being.

'Then I was for a long time in the shape of that hawk, so that I outlived all those races who had invaded Ireland. However, the sons of Mu took this island by force from the Tuatha Dé Danann. Then I was in the shape of that hawk in which I had been, and was in the hollow of a tree on a river.

'There I fasted for three days and three nights, when sleep fell upon me, and I passed into the shape of a river-salmon there and then. Then God put me into the river so that I was in it. Once more I felt happy and was vigorous and well-fed, and my swimming was good, and I used to escape from every danger and from every snare – to wit, from the hands of fishermen, and from the claws of hawks, and from fishing spears – so that the scars which each one of them left are still on me.

'Once, however, when God, my help, deemed it time, and when the beasts were pursuing me, and every

fisherman in every pool knew me, the fisherman of
Cairell, the king of that land, caught me and took me
with him to Cairell's wife, who had a desire for fish.
Indeed I remember it; the man put me on a gridiron and
roasted me. And the queen desired me and ate me by
herself, so that I was in her womb. Again, I remember
the time that I was in her womb, and what each one
said to her in the house, and what was done in Ireland
during that time. I also remember when speech came to
me, as it comes to any man, and I knew all that was
being done in Ireland, and I was a seer; and a name was
given to me – to wit, Tuan, son of Cairell. Thereupon
Patrick came with the faith to Ireland. Then I was of
great age; and I was baptized, and alone believed in the
King of all things with his elements.'

Irish, 15th century (59)

THE PROPHECY OF GWENC'LAN

I

When the sun sets, when the tide comes in, I sing
  on the threshold of my home.
When I was young, I sung; now I'm old, I still
  sing.

I sing at night, I sing during the day, and still, I
    am sad.

If I lower my head, if I'm sad, it's not without
    reason.

It's not that I am afraid, I don't fear being killed.

It's not that I am afraid, I've lived long enough.

When I'm not sought, I will be found; and when
    I'm sought, I am not found.

Never mind what will happen, what must be, will
    be.

Everyone must die three times before resting at
    last.

II

I see the wild boar coming out of the wood; he
    limps a lot; his foot is injured,

The mouth wide open and full of blood, and his
    hair white with age;

He is surrounded by his young snorting with
    hunger.

I see the sea horse coming towards him, such to
    make the seashore tremble with fright.

He is as white as shining snow; he wears silver
    horns on his forehead

The water is boiling underneath him, from the
   thunder of his nostrils.
Two sea horses surround him, as near as the grass
   by the pond.
Hold on! Hold on! Sea horse; hit him on the head;
   hit him hard, hit him!
The bare feet slide in the blood! Harder still! Go
   on, hit him! Harder still!
I see the blood makes a river! Hit him hard! Go on,
   hit him! Harder still!
I see the blood rise to his knees! I see the blood
   makes a lake!
Harder still! Go on, hit him! Harder still! You will
   rest tomorrow.
Hit him hard! Hit him hard, sea horse! Hit him on
   the head! Hit him hard! Hit him! —

III

As I was sleeping peacefully in my cold tomb,
   I heard the eagle calling in the middle of the
   night.
He was calling his young and all the birds of the
   sky.
And as he was calling, he was saying:

– Quick get up quickly on both your wings!
It's not rotten flesh from dogs and sheep we need;
    it's Christian flesh! –
– Old sea crow, tell me, what are you holding
    here?
– I hold the head of the Chief of the Army; I want
    to have his two red eyes.
I tear out both his eyes because he tore yours.
– What about you, fox, tell me, what are you
    holding here?
– I hold his heart that was as false as mine.
He desired your death and made you die long ago.
– And what about you, toad, tell me, what are you
    doing here, by the corner of his mouth?
– Me, I am posted here to wait for his soul when it
    comes by,
It will stay in me for as long as I live, as
    punishment of the crime he committed.
Against the Bard who does not live anymore
    between Roc'h-allaz and Porzgwenn.

Breton, 5th century CE (60)

STORIES,
DEEDS AND
PARABLES

THE VOYAGE OF BRAN, SON OF FEBAL, AND HIS EXPEDITION

A story about reality and its limits. Bran's journey through and beyond time takes him to a magical, luxurious island. Driven by homesickness to return to Ireland, he finds that so much time has passed that he, his comrades and his journey are now only mythology, so he sails away again.

And he saw an island. He rows round about it, and a large host was gaping and laughing. They were all looking at Bran and his people, but would not stay to converse with them. They continued to give forth gusts of laughter at them. Bran sent one of his people on the island. He ranged himself with the others, and was gaping at them like the other men of the island. He kept rowing round about the island. Whenever his man came past Bran, his comrades would address him. But he would not converse with them, but would only look at them and gape at them. The name of this island is the Island of Joy. Thereupon they left him there.

It was not long thereafter when they reached the Land of Women. They saw the leader of the women at the port. Said the chief of the women: 'Come hither on

land; O Bran son of Febal! Welcome is thy advent!' Bran
did not venture to go on shore. The woman throws a
ball of thread to Bran straight over his face. Bran put his
hand on the ball, which clave to his palm. The thread of
the ball was in the woman's hand, and she pulled the
coracle towards the port. Thereupon they went into a
large house, in which was a bed for every couple, even
thrice nine beds. The food that was put on every dish
vanished not from them. It seemed a year to them that
they were there – it chanced to be many years. No
savour was wanting to them.

Home-sickness seized one of them, even Nechtan the
son of Collbran. His kindred kept praying Bran that he
should go to Ireland with him. The woman said to them
their going would make them rue. However, they went,
and the woman said that none of them should touch the
land, and that they should visit and take with them the
man whom they had left in the Island of Joy.

Then they went until they arrived at a gathering at
Srub Brain. The men asked of them who it was came
over the sea. Said Bran: 'I am Bran the son of Febal,'
saith he. However, the other saith: 'We do not know
such a one, though the Voyage of Bran is in our ancient
stories.'

The man leaps from them out of the coracle. As soon

as he touched the earth of Ireland, forthwith he was a heap of ashes, as though he had been in the earth for many hundred years. 'Twas then that Bran sang this quatrain:

'For Collbran's son great was the folly
To lift his hand against age,
Without any one casting a wave of pure water
Over Nechtan, Collbran's son.'

Thereupon, to the people of the gathering Bran told all his wanderings from the beginning until that time. And he wrote these quatrains in Ogam, and then bade them farewell. And from that hour his wanderings are not known.

Irish, c1100 (61)

FROM THE STORY OF TALIESIN

Taliesin was a 6th-century Welsh bardic poet. His name means 'Behold, a Radiant Brow.' The story tells of his being found as a child, in a leather bag hung on a pole over a weir, and of how he received his name. The story illustrates the Celtic resonance with all of nature, and of the almost shamanistic ability to transform from a human being to an animal.

In times past there lived in Penllyn a man of gentle lineage named Tegid Voel, and his dwelling was in the midst of the lake Tegid, and his wife was called Caridwen. And there was born to him of his wife a son named Morvran ab Tegid, and also a daughter named Creirwy, the fairest maiden in the world was she; and they had a brother, the most ill-favoured man in the world, Avagddu. Now Caridwen, his mother, thought that he was not likely to be admitted among men of noble birth, by reason of his ugliness, unless he had some exalted merits or knowledge. For it was in the beginning of Arthur's time and of the Round Table.

So she resolved, according to the arts of the books of the Fferyllt, to boil a cauldron of Inspiration and Science for her son, that his reception might be honourable because of his knowledge of the mysteries of the future state of the world.

Then she began to boil the cauldron, which from the beginning of its boiling might not cease to boil for a year and a day, until three blessed drops were obtained of the grace of Inspiration.

And she put Gwion Bach the son of Gwreang of Llanfair in Caereinion, in Powys, to stir the cauldron, and a blind man named Morda to kindle the fire beneath it, and she charged them that they should not suffer it to cease boiling for the space of a year and a day. And she herself, according to the books of the astronomers, and in planetary hours, gathered every day of all charm-bearing herbs. And one day, towards the end of the year, as Caridwen was culling plants and making incantations, it chanced that three drops of the charmed liquor flew out of the cauldron and fell upon the finger of Gwion Bach. And by reason of their great heat he put his finger to his mouth, and the instant he put those marvel-working drops into his mouth, he foresaw everything that was to come, and perceived that his chief care must be to guard against the wiles of Caridwen, for vast was her skill. And in very great fear he fled towards his own land. And the cauldron burst in two, because all the liquor within it except the three charm-bearing drops was poisonous, so that the horses of Gwyddno Grainier were poisoned by the water of the stream into which the liquor of the cauldron ran, and the confluence of that stream was called the Poison of the Horses of Gwyddno from that time forth.

Thereupon came in Caridwen and saw all the toil of the whole year lost. And she seized a billet of wood and struck the blind Morda on the head until one of his eyes fell out upon his cheek. And he said, 'Wrongfully hast thou disfigured me, for I am innocent. Thy loss was not because of me.' 'Thou speakest truth,' said Caridwen, 'it was Gwion Bach who robbed me.'

And she went forth after him, running. And he saw her, and changed himself into a hare and fled. But she changed herself into a greyhound and turned him. And he ran towards a river, and became a fish. And she in the form of an otter-bitch chased him under the water, until he was fain to turn himself into a bird of the air. She, as a hawk, followed him and gave him no rest in the sky. And just as she was about to stoop upon him, and he was in fear of death, he espied a heap of winnowed wheat on the floor of a barn, and he dropped among the wheat, and turned himself into one of the grains. Then she transformed herself into a high-crested black hen, and went to the wheat and scratched it with her feet, and found him out and swallowed him. And, as the story says, she bore him nine months, and when she was delivered of him, she could not find it in her heart to kill him, by reason of his beauty. So she wrapped him in a leathern bag, and cast him into the sea to the mercy of God, on the twenty-ninth day of April.

And at that time the weir of Gwyddno was on the strand between Dyvi and Aberystwyth, near to his own castle, and the value of an hundred pounds was taken in that weir every May eve. And in those days Gwyddno had an only son named Elphin, the most hapless of youths, and the most needy. And it grieved his father sore, for he thought that he was born in an evil hour. And by the advice of his council, his father had granted him the drawing of the weir that year, to see if good luck would ever befall him, and to give him something wherewith to begin the world.

And the next day when Elphin went to look, there was nothing in the weir. But as he turned back he perceived the leathern bag upon a pole of the weir. Then said one of the weir-ward unto Elphin, 'Thou wast never unlucky until to-night, and now thou hast destroyed the virtues of the weir, which always yielded the value of an hundred pounds every May eve, and to-night there is nothing but this leathern skin within it.' 'How now,' said Elphin, 'there may be therein the value of an hundred pounds.' Well, they took up the leathern bag, and he who opened it saw the forehead of the boy, and said to Elphin, 'Behold a radiant brow!'

'Taliesin be he called,' said Elphin. And he lifted the boy in his arms, and lamenting his mischance, he placed him sorrowfully behind him. And he made his horse amble gently, that before had been trotting, and he carried him as softly as if he had been sitting in the easiest chair in the world. And presently the boy made a Consolation and praise to Elphin, and foretold honour to Elphin; and the Consolation was as you may see:

'Fair Elphin, cease to lament!
Let no one be dissatisfied with his own,
To despair will bring no advantage.
No man sees what supports him;
The prayer of Cynllo will not be in vain;
God will not violate his promise.
Never in Gwyddno's weir
Was there such good luck as this night.
Fair Elphin, dry thy cheeks!
Being too sad will not avail.
Although thou thinkest thou hast no gain,
Too much grief will bring thee no good;
Nor doubt the miracles of the Almighty:
Although I am but little, I am highly gifted.
From seas, and from mountains,
And from the depths of rivers,
God brings wealth to the fortunate man.
Elphin of lively qualities,
Thy resolution is unmanly;
Thou must not be over sorrowful:
Better to trust in God than to forbode ill.
Weak and small as I am,
On the foaming beach of the ocean,
In the day of trouble I shall be

Of more service to thee than three hundred
    salmon.
Elphin of notable qualities,
Be not displeased at thy misfortune;
Although reclined thus weak in my bag,
There lies a virtue in my tongue.
While I continue thy protector
Thou hast not much to fear;
Remembering the names of the Trinity,
None shall be able to harm thee.'

And this was the first poem that Taliesin ever sang,
being to console Elphin in his grief for that the produce
of the weir was lost, and, what was worse, that all the
world would consider that it was through his fault and
ill-luck.

Welsh, 14th century (62)

THE ANCIENTS OF THE WORLD

There was once an Eagle living in the woods of
Gwernabwy: he and his mate had young ones till the
ninth generation and far beyond that; then the old
mother eagle died, leaving her husband a lonely

widower, without anyone to console and cheer him in his old age. In the sadness of his heart he thought it would be well if he married an old widow of his own age. Hearing of the old Owl of Cwm Cawlyd, he took it into his head to make her his second wife, but before doing so, being anxious not to degrade his race, he determined to make enquiries about her.

He had an old friend, older than himself, the Stag of Rhedynfre, in Gwent. He went to him and asked the age of the old Owl. The Stag answered him thus:

'Seest thou, my friend, this oak by which I lie? It is now but a withered stump, without leaves or branches, but I remember seeing it an acorn on the top of the chief tree of this forest. An oak is three hundred years in growing, and after that three hundred years in its strength and prime, and after that three hundred years in returning unto earth. Upwards of sixty years of the last hundred of this oak are passed, and the Owl has been old since I first remember her. Nor does anyone of my kindred know her age. But I have a friend who is much older than I, the Salmon of Llyn Llifon. Go to him and ask him if he knows aught of the age and history of the old Owl.'

The Eagle went to the Salmon, who answered him thus: 'I have a year over my head for every gem on my skin and for every egg in my roe, but the Owl was old when first I remember her. But I have a friend who is much older than I, the Ousel of Cilgwri. Haply he knows more about the Owl than I do.'

The Eagle went and found the Ousel sitting on a hard flint, and asked him if he knew aught of the age and history of the Owl. The Ousel answering, said: 'Seest thou this flint on which I sit? I have seen it so large that it would have taken three hundred yoke of the largest oxen to move it, and it has never been worn away save by my cleaning my beak upon it once every night before going to sleep, and striking the tip of my wing against it after rising in the morning. Yet never have I known the Owl younger or older than she is to-day. But I have a friend who is much older than I, the Toad of Cors Fochno. Go to him and ask him if he knows aught of the age and history of the Owl.'

The Eagle went to the Toad, who answered him thus.

'I never eat any food save the dust of the earth, and I never eat half enough to satisfy me. Seest thou the great hills around this bog? I have seen the place where they stand level ground. I have eaten all the earth they contain, though I eat so little for fear lest the mould of the earth should be consumed before my death. Yet never have I known the Owl anything else but an old grey hag who cried to-whit-to-whoo in the woods in the long winter nights, and scared children with her voice even as she does to-day.'

Then the Eagle saw he could marry her without bringing disgrace or degradation on his tribe. And so it was from the courtship of the Eagle that it was known which were the oldest creatures in the world. They are the Eagle of Gwernabwy, the Stag of Rhedynfre, the Salmon of Llyn Llifon, the Ousel of Cilgwri, the Toad of Cors Fochno, and the Owl of Cwm Cawlyd, and the oldest of them all is the Owl.

Welsh, traditional (63)

THE SECOND BATTLE OF MAD TUIRED

Then after the battle was won and the slaughter had been cleaned away, the Morrigan, the daughter of Ernmas, proceeded to announce the battle and the great victory which had occurred there to the royal heights of Ireland and to its *sid*-hosts, to its chief waters and to its river mouths. And that is the reason Badb still relates great deeds. 'Have you any news?' everyone asked her then.

'Peace up to heaven.
Heaven down to earth.
Earth beneath heaven,
Strength in each,
A cup very full,
Full of honey;
Mead in abundance.
Summer in winter. ...
Peace up to heaven ...'

She also prophesied the end of the world, foretelling every evil that would occur then, and every disease and every vengeance; and she chanted the following poem:

'I shall not see a world
Which will be dear to me:
Summer without blossoms,
Cattle will be without milk,
Women without modesty,
Men without valour.
Conquests without a king ...
Woods without mast.
Sea without produce. ...
False judgements of old men.

False precedents of lawyers,
Every man a betrayer.
Every son a reaver.
The son will go to the bed of his father,
The father will go to the bed of his son.
Each his brother's brother-in-law.
He will not seek any woman outside his house. ...
An evil time,
Son will deceive his father,
Daughter will deceive ...'

Irish, 9th century (64)

THE BIRDS OF RHIANNON

*Wirt Sikes recounts two legends illustrating
the formative place of music in Celtic
mythology and folklore.*

The Birds of Rhiannon sang until the Angels of heaven
came to listen to them; and it was from their songs that
were first obtained vocal song and instrumental music;
vocal song being that which is sung by the lips to
melody and harp.

Seven men only had escaped from a certain battle

with the Irish, and they were bidden by their dying chief to cut off his head and bear it to London and bury it with the face towards France. Various were the adventures they encountered while obeying this injunction. At Harlech they stopped to rest, and sat down to eat and drink. 'And there came three birds, and began singing unto them a certain song, and all the songs they had ever heard were unpleasant compared thereto; and the birds seemed to them to be at a great distance from them over the sea, yet they appeared as distinct as if they were close by; and at this repast they continued seven years.' [Lady Charlotte Guest's *Mabinogion*, 1877.] This enchanting fancy reappears in the local story of Shon ap Shenkin, which was related to me by a farmer's wife near the reputed scene of the legend. Pant Shon Shenkin has already been mentioned as a famous centre for Carmarthenshire fairies. The story of Taffy ap Sion and this of Shon ap Shenkin were probably one and the same at some period in their career, although they are now distinct. Shon ap Shenkin was a young man who lived hard by Pant Shon Shenkin. As he was going afield early one fine summer's morning he heard a little bird singing, in a most enchanting strain, on a tree close by his path. Allured by the melody he sat down under the tree until the music ceased, when he arose and looked about him. What was his surprise at observing that the tree, which was green and full of life when he sat down, was now withered and barkless! Filled with astonishment he returned to the farmhouse which he had left, as he supposed, a few minutes before; but it also was changed, grown older, and covered with ivy. In the doorway stood an old man whom he had never before seen; he at once asked the old man what he wanted there. 'What do I want here?' ejaculated the old man, reddening angrily; 'that's a pretty question Who are you that dare to insult me in my own house?' 'In your own house? How is this? where's my father and mother, whom I left here a few minutes since, whilst I have been listening to the charming music under yon tree, which, when I rose, was withered and leafless?' 'Under the tree! – music! what's your name?' 'Shon ap Shenkin.' 'Alas, poor Shon, and is this indeed you?' cried the old man. 'I often heard my grandfather, your father, speak of you, and long did he bewail your absence. Fruitless inquiries were made for you; but old Catti Maddock of Brechfa said you were under the power of the fairies, and would not be released until the last sap of that sycamore tree would be dried up. Embrace me, my dear uncle, for you are my uncle – embrace your nephew.' With this the old man extended his arms, but before the two men could embrace, poor Shon ap Shenkin crumbled into dust on the doorstep.

Welsh, traditional (65)

ADVICE TO A PRINCE

There was a meeting of the three provinces of Ireland held about this time in Teamhair, so they could find some person to give the High Kingship of Ireland to; for they thought it a pity the Hill of the Lordship of Ireland, that is Teamhair, to be without the rule of a king on it, and the tribes to be without a king's government to judge their houses. For the men of Ireland had been without the government of a High King over them since the death of Conaire at Da Derga's Inn.

And the kings that met now at the court of Cairbre Niafer were Ailell and Maeve of Connaught, and Curoi, and Tigernach, son of Luchta, king of Tuathmumain, and Finn, son of Ross, king of Leinster. But they would not ask the men of Ulster to help them in choosing a king, for they were all of them against the men of Ulster.

There was a bull-feast made ready then, the same way as the time Conaire was chosen, to find out who was the best man to get the kingship.

After a while the dreamer screamed out in his sleep, and told what he saw to the kings. And what he saw this time, was a young strong man, with high looks, and with two red stripes on his body, and he sitting over the pillow of a man that was wasting away in Emain Macha. A message was sent then with this account to Emain Macha. The men of Ulster were gathered at that time about Cuchulain, that was on his sick-bed. The messenger told his story to Conchubar and to the chief men of Ulster.

'There is a young man of good race and good birth with us now that answers to that account,' said Conchubar; 'that is Lugaid of the Red Stripes, son of Clothru, daughter of Eochaid Feidlech, the pupil of Cuchulain; and he is sitting by his pillow within, caring him, for he is on his sick-bed.'

And when it was told Cuchulain that messengers were come for Lugaid, to make him King in Teamhair, he rose up and began to advise him, and it is what he said:

'Do not be a frightened man in a battle; do not be light-minded, hard to reach, or proud. Do not be ungentle, or

hasty, or passionate; do not be overcome with the
drunkenness of great riches, like a flea that is drowned
in the ale of a king's house. Do not scatter many feasts
to strangers; do not visit mean people that cannot
receive you as a king. Do not let wrongful possession
stand because it has lasted long; but let witnesses be
searched to know who is the right owner of land. Let
the tellers of history tell truth before you; let the lands
of brothers and their increase be set down in their
lifetime; if a family has increased in its branches, is it
not from the one stem they are come? Let them be
called up, let the old claims be established by oaths; let
the heir be left in lawful possession of the place his
fathers lived in; let strangers be driven off it by force.

'Do not use too many words. Do not speak noisily;
do not mock, do not give insults, do not make little of
old people. Do not think ill of any one; do not ask what
is hard to give. Let you have a law of lending, a law of
oppression, a law of pledging. Be obedient to the advice
of the wise; keep in mind the advice of the old. Be a
follower of the rules of your fathers. Do not be cold-
hearted to friends; be strong towards your enemies; do
not give evil for evil in your battles. Do not be given to
too much talking. Do not speak any harm of others. Do
not waste, do not scatter, do not do away with what is
your own. When you do wrong, take the blame of it; do

not give up the truth for any man. Do not be trying to be first, that way you will not be jealous; do not be an idler, that you may not be weak; do not ask too much, that you may not be thought little of. Are you willing to follow this advice, my son?'

Then Lugaid answered Cuchulain, and it is what he said: 'As long as all goes well, I will keep to your words, and every one will know that there is nothing wanting in me; all will be done that can be done.'

Then Lugaid went away with the messengers to Teamhair, and he was made king, and he slept in Teamhair that night. And after that all the people that had gathered there went to their own homes.

Irish, 7th–8th century (66)

DREAMING AND THE SOUL

Hugh Miller, in *My Schools and Schoolmasters* (ch. vi), records a story told him by his cousin at Gruids, Sutherland. He communicated to me, says Miller, a tradition illustrative of the Celtic theory of dreaming, of which I have since often thought. 'Two young men had been spending the early portion of a warm summer day in exactly such a scene as that in which he communicated the anecdote. There was an ancient ruin beside them, separated, however, from the mossy bank on which they sat, by a slender runnel, across which there lay, immediately over a miniature cascade, a few withered grass stalks. Overcome by the heat of the day, one of the young men fell asleep; his companion watched drowsily beside him; when all at once the watcher was aroused to attention by seeing a little indistinct form, scarce larger than a humble-bee, issue from the mouth of the sleeping man, and, leaping upon the moss, move downwards to the runnel, which it crossed along the withered grass stalks, and then disappeared amid the interstices of the ruin. Alarmed by what he saw, the watcher hastily shook his companion by the shoulder, and awoke him; though, with all his haste, the little cloud-like creature, still more rapid in its movements, issued from the interstice into which it had gone, and, flying across the runnel, instead of creeping along the grass stalks and over the sward, as before, it re-entered the mouth of the sleeper, just as he was in the act of awakening. 'What is the matter with you?' said the watcher, greatly alarmed, 'What ails you?' 'Nothing ails me,' replied the other; 'but you have robbed me of a most delightful dream. I dreamed I was walking through a fine rich country, and came at length to the shores of a noble river; and, just where the clear water went thundering down a precipice, there was a bridge all of silver, which I crossed; and then, entering a noble palace, on the opposite side, I saw great heaps of gold and jewels, and I was just going to load myself with treasure, when you rudely awoke me, and I lost all.'

Celtic, traditional (67)

NATURE

THE NATURAL AND
SUPERNATURAL WORLD

The natural world is that which continues and develops
from the creative impulse. The supernatural is that part
of the natural not yet comprehended by men. The Great
God Above All is a Being composed of the collective
souls of men departed to godhood. For it is written in
times of yore that God died in the effort of creation, but
a New God is being reformed. The whole of creation
and life, as it manifests, is the effect of the Old God
being transmuted into a New One.

Pre-Christian, 2nd century BCE–1st century CE (68)

THE SCHOLAR AND HIS CAT

*A 9th–10th-century poem, sometimes called
'The Monk and his Cat', playfully illustrates
the Celtic ideal of the kind of relationship to be
enjoyed between humans and animals, and
that human beings can regain something of the
deeper and lost instincts of their own animal
origins. The poem, by an unknown Irish monk,
a student of the Monastery of St Paul,*

*Carinthia, was found written in the margins
of a copy of St Paul's Epistles.*

I and Pangur Bán, my cat
'Tis a like task we are at;
Hunting mice is his delight
Hunting words I sit all night.

Better far than praise of men
'Tis to sit with book and pen;
Pangur bears me no ill will,
He too plies his simple skill.

'Tis a merry thing to see
At our tasks how glad are we,
When at home we sit and find
Entertainment to our mind.

Oftentimes a mouse will stray
In the hero Pangur's way:
Oftentimes my keen thought set
Takes a meaning in its net.

'Gainst the wall he sets his eye
Full and fierce and sharp and sly;

'Gainst the wall of knowledge I
All my little wisdom try.

When a mouse darts from its den,
O how glad is Pangur then!
O what gladness do I prove
When I solve the doubts I love!

So in peace our tasks we ply,
Pangur Bán, my cat, and I;
In our arts we find our bliss,
I have mine and he has his.

Practice every day has made
Pangur perfect in his trade;
I get wisdom day and night
Turning darkness into light.

Irish, c9th century (69)

TREES IN BATTLE

For a leader of Gwydion's magical attainments there was
no need of standing troops. He could call battalions into
being with a charm, and dismiss them when they were

no longer needed. The name of the battle shows what he did on this occasion; and the bard Taliesin adds his testimony:

> 'I have been in the battle of Godeu, with Lieu and Gwydion,
> They changed the forms of the elementary trees and sedges.'

In a poem devoted to it he describes in detail what happened. The trees and grasses, he tells us, hurried to the fight: the alders led the van, but the willows and the quickens came late, and the birch, though courageous, took long in arraying himself; the elm stood firm in the centre of the battle, and would not yield a foot; heaven and earth trembled before the advance of the oak-tree, that stout door-keeper against an enemy; the heroic holly and the hawthorn defended themselves with their spikes; the heather kept off the enemy on every side, and the broom was well to the front, but the fern was plundered, and the furze did not do well; the stout, lofty pine, the intruding pear-tree, the gloomy ash, the bashful chestnut-tree, the prosperous beech, the long-enduring poplar, the scarce plum-tree, the shelter-seeking privet and woodbine, the wild, foreign laburnum; 'the bean, bearing in its

shade an army of phantoms'; rose-bush, raspberry, ivy,
cherry-tree, and medlar, all took their parts.

Irish, c1160 (70)

PRIMITIVE NATURE WORSHIP

Landscape and nature related to as if they were human,
personalities with power.

Amairgin, the poet of the Milesians, on invading
Ireland:

'I invoke the land of Ireland
Shining, shining sea!
Fertile, fertile mountain!
Wooded vale!
Abundant river, abundant in waters!
Fish abounding lake!
Fish abounding sea!
Fertile earth!
Irruption of fish! Fish there!
Bird under wave! Great fish!
Crab hole! Irruption of fish!
Fish abounding sea!'

Celtic, pre-Christian (71)

HEALING HERBS, CHARMS AND WISE WOMEN

This is *dwareen* (knapweed) and what you have to do with this is to put it down, with other herbs, and with a bit of three-penny sugar, and to boil it and to drink it for pains in the bones, and don't be afraid but it will cure you. Sure the Lord put it in the world for curing.

And this is corn-corn (small aromatic tansy); it's very good for the heart – boiled like the others.

This is *atair-talam* (wild camomile), the father of all herbs – the father of the ground. This is very hard to pull, and when you go for it, you must have a black-handled knife.

And this is *camal-buide* (loosestrife) that will keep all bad things away.

This is *fearaban* (water buttercup) and it's good for every bone of your body.

This is *dub-cosac* (lichen), that's good for the heart, very good for a sore heart. Here are the *sianlus* (plantain) and the *garblus* (dandelion) and these would cure the wide world,

The *bainne-bo-bliatain* (wood anemone) is good for the headache, if you put the leaves of it on your head. But as for the *us-mor* it's best not to have anything to do with that.

The wild parsnip is good for gravel, and for heartbeat there's nothing so good as dandelion. There was a woman I knew used to boil it down, and she'd throw out what was left on the grass. And there was a fleet of turkeys about the house and they used to be picking it up. And at Christmas they killed one of them, and when it was cut open they found a new heart growing in it with the dint of the dandelion.

For a swelling in the throat it's an herb would be used, or for the evil a poultice you'd make of herbs. But for a pain in the ribs or in the head, it's a charm you should use, and to whisper it into a bit of tow, and to put it on the mouth of whoever would have the pain, and that would take it away. There's a herb called rif in your own garden that is good for cures. And this is a good charm to say in Irish:

> 'A quiet woman.
> A rough man.
> The Son of God.
> The husk of the flax.'

Irish, traditional (72)

ANIMALS

COWS, PIGS AND LAMBS

The worst form a monster can take is a cow or a pig. But as to a lamb, you may always be sure a lamb is honest. A pig is the worst shape they can take. I wouldn't like to meet anything in the shape of a pig in the night.

COCKS

And a black cock everyone likes to have in their house – a March cock it should be. If you can have it from a March clutch, and the next year if you can have another cock from a March clutch from that one, it's the best. And if you go late out of the house, and that there is something outside it would be bad to meet, that cock will crow before you'll go out.

HARES

As to hares, there's something queer about them, and there's some that it's dangerous to meddle with, and that can go into any form where they like. Sure, Mrs Madden is after having a young son, and it has a harelip. But she says that she doesn't remember that ever she met a hare or looked at one. But if she did, she had a right to rip a small bit of the seam of her dress or her petticoat, and then it would have no power to hurt her at all. … As to hares, they're the biggest fairies of all.

CATS

As to cats, they're a class in themselves. And it's certain that once one night every year, in the month of November, all the cats of the whole country round gather together there and fight. My own two cats were nearly dead for days after it last year, and the neighbours told me the same of theirs. There was a woman had a cat and she would feed it at the table before any other one; and if it did not get the first meat that was cooked, the hair would rise up as high as that. Well, there were priests came to dinner one day, and when they were helped the first, the hair rose up on the cat's back. And one of them said to the woman it was a queer thing to give in to a cat the way she did, and that it was a foolish thing to be giving it the first of the food. So when it heard that, it walked out of the house, and never came into it again.

There's something not right about cats. They're good to catch mice and rats, but just let them come in and out of the house for that; they're about their own business all the time. And in the old times they could talk. Cats were serpents, and they were made into cats at the time, I suppose, of some change in the world. That's why they're hard to kill and why it's dangerous to meddle with them. If you annoy a cat it might claw you or bite you in a way that would put poison in you, and that would be the serpent's tooth.

You should never be too attentive to a cat, but just to be civil and to give it its share.

RATS

Rats are very bad, because a rat if one got the chance would do his best to bite you, and I wouldn't like at all to get the bite of a rat. But weasels are serpents, and if they would spit at any part of your body it would fester, and you would get blood poisoning within two hours.

WEASELS

Weasels are not right, no more than cats; and I'm not sure about foxes. It is wrong to insult a weasel, and if you pelt them or shoot them they will watch for you forever to ruin you. For they are enchanted and understand all things. And to see a weasel passing the road before you, there's nothing in the world like that to bring you all sorts of good luck.

HEDGEHOGS

The granyog (hedgehog) will do no harm to chickens or the like; but if he will get into an orchard he will stick an apple on every thorn, and away with him to a scalp with them to be eating through the winter. I met with a granyog one day on the mountain, and that I may never sin, he was running up the side of it as fast as a race-horse.

Irish, traditional (73)

DEATH

I AM GOING HOME

Celtic tradition does not see death as a
destructive termination of life, but a powerful
and ultimate experience of life. In Celtic
spirituality the world of eternity is inseparable
from the world of nature. Dying is both wholly
natural and wholly mysterious.

I am going home with thee, to thy home, to thy
    home,
I am going home with thee, to thy home of winter.
I am going home with thee, to thy home of
    autumn, of spring and summer.
I am going home with thee, thy child of my love,
    to thy eternal bed, to thy perpetual sleep.

Scottish, traditional (74)

THE BUTTERFLY AS THE SOUL
OF THE DEAD

The soul is at times thought to assume the form of a
butterfly, *dearbadan Dé, tarmachan Dé* being the
Highland names; they are in part god-names. The Irish
féiliocán, the Manx *follican,* 'butterfly,' do not show the

god-soul in the name, but there is an Irish legend as to a priest who came to disbelieve that men had souls. 'Who ever saw a soul?' he would say. 'If you can show me one I will believe.' All the king's sons were on his side, but at last a mysterious child comes on the scene and shows him that if we have life though we cannot see it, we may also have a soul though it is invisible. He had met at last one who believed, and having told the child his story he bade him watch, 'for a living thing will soar up from my body as I die, and you will then know that my soul has ascended into the presence of God'. This was to be a sign that his previous teaching was a lie. His death is then described, and when his agony seemed to cease, the child, who was watching, 'saw a beautiful living creature, with four snow-white wings', mount from the dead man's body into the air, and go fluttering round his head. So he ran to bring the scholars; and when they all knew it was the soul of their master, they watched with wonder and awe, until it passed from sight into the clouds. And this was the first butterfly that was ever seen in Ireland; and now all men know that the butterflies are the souls of the dead waiting for the moment when they may enter Purgatory, and so pass through torture to purification and peace. But the schools of Ireland were quite deserted after that time, for people said, what is the use of going so far to learn when the wisest man in all Ireland did not know if he had a soul till he was near losing it; and was only saved at last through the simple belief of a little child?

Celtic, traditional (75)

DEATH

St Oran, on being interred alive:

> Death is no wonder
> Nor is Hell as it is said.
> Death is nothing strange,
> Nor Hell as has been said;
> Good will not perish,
> Nor evil be unpunished.

Celtic, traditional (76)

THE UNQUIET DEAD

A good many years ago when I was but beginning my study of the folk-lore of belief, I wrote somewhere that if by an impossible miracle every trace and memory of

Christianity could be swept out of the world, it would not shake or destroy at all the belief of the people of Ireland in the invisible world, the cloud of witnesses, in immortality and the life to come. For them the veil between things seen and unseen has hardly thickened since those early days of the world when the sons of God mated with the daughters of men; when angels spoke with Abraham in Hebron or with Columcille in the oakwoods of Derry, or when as an old man at my own gate told me they came and visited the Fianna, the old heroes of Ireland, 'because they were so nice and so respectable'. Ireland has through the centuries kept continuity of vision, the vision it is likely all nations possessed in the early days of faith. Here in Connacht there is no doubt as to the continuance of life after death. The spirit wanders for a while in that intermediate region to which mystics and theologians have given various names, and should it return and become visible those who loved it will not be afraid, but will, as I have already told, put a light in the window to guide the mother home to her child, or go out into the barley gardens in the hope of meeting a son. And if the message brought seems hardly worth the hearing, we may call to mind what Frederic Myers wrote of more instructed ghosts:

'If it was absurd to listen to Kepler because he bade the planets move in no perfect circles but in undignified ellipses, because he hastened and slackened from hour to hour what ought to be a heavenly body's ideal and unwavering speed; is it not absurder still to refuse to listen to these voices from afar, because they come stammering and wandering as in a dream confusedly instead of with a trumpet's call? Because spirits that bending to earth may undergo perhaps an earthly bewilderment and suffer unknown limitations, and half remember and half forget?'

And should they give the message more clearly who knows if it would be welcome? For the old Scotch story goes that when S. Columcille's brother Dobhran rose up from his grave and said, 'Hell is not so bad as people say,' the Saint cried out, 'Clay, clay on Dobhran!' before he could tell any more.

Irish, traditional (77)

THE CORPSE CANDLE

A very commonly received opinion, that within the diocese of St David's, a short space before death, a light is seen proceeding from the house, and sometimes, as has been asserted, from the very bed where the sick

person lies, and pursues its way to the church where he
or she is to be interred, precisely in the same track in
which the funeral is afterwards to follow.

> All under the stars, and beneath the green tree,
> All over the sward, and along the cold lea,
> A little blue flame a-fluttering came;
> It came from the churchyard for you or for me.
>
> I sit by the cradle, my baby's asleep,
> And rocking the cradle, I wonder and weep.
> O little blue light in the dead of the night,
> O prithee, O prithee, no nearer to creep.
>
> Why follow the church-path, why steal you this
>   way?
> Why halt in your journey, on threshold why stay?
> With flicker and flare, why dance up the stair?
> O I would! O I would! it were dawning of day.
> All under the stars, and along the green lane,
>
> Unslaked by the dew, and unquenched by the
>   rain,
> Of little flames blue to the churchyard steal two,
> The soul of my baby! now from me is ta'an.

Welsh, 18th century (78)

AN IRISH BLESSING

May the path rise to meet you.
May you always have the wind at your back.
May the sun shine warmly in your face.
and the rain fall mildly amid the fields;
and until we meet again,
may gods keep you in their hands.

The Shamrock of St Patrick

REFERENCES

1. *The Book of Invasions*.
2. *Altus Prosator*, authored by Columba and written in Hiberno-Latin.
3. *The Barddas of Iolo Morganwg*.
4. *Tenga Bithnua*, in *The King of Mysteries*, Four Courts Press, 1998.
5. *Survivals in Belief Among the Celts*, George Henderson, 1911.
6. *Mestre Jehan an Archer Coz*, trans. Nadège Phillipson.
7. *The Kolbrin Bible*, Book of Lucius (LUC 1:11).
8. *The Kolbrin Bible*, Book of the Silver Bough (SVB 6:3–4) and Book of Origins (OGS 9:34).
9. *The Kolbrin Bible*, Book of the Silver Bough (SVB 8:14–16).
10. 'The Song of Trust', from *English and Scottish Popular Ballads*, Francis James Child (compiled 1882–98).
11. Traditional, recovered by the Rev. Dr Kenneth Macleod.
12. *The Religion of the Ancient Celts*, J. A. MacCulloch, 1911.
13. Evan James. Traditionally the national anthem of Wales, music by James James.

14. See 12.
15. Report of the Highland Society on the poems of Ossian.
16. Attributed to Columba.
17. 'Coming Of Age', *The Book Of Rites,* Sìtheag Nic Trantham bean Bochanan.
18. See 17.
19. The content of the rite suggests an early usage within Celtic Christianity, thus before the Synod of Whitby. The practice was popular in Scotland in the 16th and 17th centuries.
20. Brigit, c452–525 CE, known also as 'The Mary of the Gael'. *A Book of Saints and Wonders,* Lady Gregory, 1906 (Internet Sacred Texts Archive).
21. *Some Aspects of Irish Literature*, Pádraic H. Pearse, trans. MacDonagh.
22. *The Carmina Gadelica*, Alexander Carmichael, 1900.
23. *Naturalis Historia*. Pliny is one of several Roman sources for Celtic religion and culture.
24. Manuscript Collection by Llywelyn Sion, a Bard of Glamorgan.
25. *The Candle of Vision*, AE (George William Russell), 1918.
26. *Book of Leinster*, c1160, trans. Whitley Stokes.

27. *Irish Fairy Tales*, James Stephens, Macmillan & Co., London, 1920.

28. See 27.

29. 'The Boyhood Deed of Fenian', *Fenian Cycle*.

30. *Myths and Legends of the Celtic Race*, Thomas Rollestone, 1911.

31. *Kolbrin Bible*, Book of the Silver Bough (SVB 3:21).

32. *Le Barzhaz Breizh*, Théodore Hersart de La Villemarqué (1815–95), trans. Nadège Phillipson.

33. The Confession of St Patrick.

34. *Ancient Legends, Mystic Charms and Superstitions of Ireland*, Lady Francesca Speranza Wilde, 1887.

35. *Kolbrin Bible*, Book of Origins (OGS 9:35).

36. *Carmina Gadelic Hymns and Incantation*, vol. I, compiled by Alexander Carmichael (1855–1910) (Internet Sacred Texts Archive).

37. See 36. Vol. II.

38. See 36.

39. See 36.

40. The author of the hymn is Broccan the Crooked, *The King of Mysteries*, Four Courts Press, 1998.

41. *A Book of Saints and Wonders,* Lady Gregory, 1906 (Internet Sacred Texts Archive).

42. See 36.

43. See 36.

44. See 36.

45. *Traditional Laws, Customs and Wisdom of the Pre-Christian Celtic People of Scotland, Wales and Ireland*, John F Wright. See: http://www.featherlessbiped.com.

46. See 45.

47. *Kolbrin Bible*, Book of Origins, 'The Maymen Lore' (OGS 10:3).

48. See 47 (OGS 10:10–11).

49. *The Black Book of Carmarthen.*

50. *Kolbrin Bible*, Book of Origins, 'The Battlebook' (OGS 9:32, 34).

51. 'Cormac's Rule', *Eriu*, vol. II, John Strachan, David Nutt, London, 1905.

52. 'Caesar: De Bello Gallico', Book VI, ch. XVI, *Celtic Myth and Legend*, Charles Squire, 1905.

53. *Books of Leinster, of Ballymote, of Lecan.*

54. *Kolbrin Bible*, Book of the Silver Bough (SVB 7:5).

55. See 54 (SVB 7:23–24).

56. See 54 (SVB 8:32).

57. 'Mongan's Frenzy', *Irish Fairy Tales*, James Stephens, Macmillan & Co., London, 1920.

58. Trans. Erynn Rowan Laurie. See: http://www.seanet.com/~inisglas.

59. 'Lives of Saints', *The Book of Lismore*, Whitley Stokes, 1890.

60. *Barzhaz Breizh*, Hersart of Villemarqué, trans. Nadège Phillipson.

61. 'The Voyage of Bran', trans. Kuno Meyer, 1895 (Internet Sacred Texts Archive).

62. Extract from 'Taliesin', *Mabinogion*, trans. Lady Guest, 1877.

63. *The Welsh Fairy Book*, W. Jenkyn Thomas, 1908.

64. *The Second Battle of Mad Tuired*, trans. Elizabeth Gray (Internet Sacred Texts Archive).

65. *British Goblins, Welsh Folk-lore, Fairy Mythology, Legends and Traditions*, Wirt Sikes, 1880.

66. *Cuchulain of Muirthemne*, Lady Augusta Gregory, 1902.

67. *Survivals in Belief Among the Celts*, George Henderson, 1911 (Internet Sacred Texts Archive).

68. *Kolbrin Bible*, Book of Origins, 'The Maymen Lore' (OSG 10:5).

69. Trans. Robert Flower.

70. 'The Victories of Light over Darkness', *Books of Leinster, of Ballymote, of Lecan*.

71. *The Religion of the Ancient Celts*, J. A. MacCulloch, 1911.

72. *Visions and Beliefs in the West of Ireland*, Lady Augusta Gregory, 1920.

73. See 72.

74. *Carmina Gadelic Hymns and Incantation*, Vol. I, compiled by Alexander Carmichael (1855–1910) (Internet Sacred Texts Archive).

75. *Survivals in Belief Among the Celts*, George Henderson, 1911 (Internet Sacred Texts Archive).

76. See 75.

77. *Visions and Beliefs in the West of Ireland*, Lady Augusta Gregory, 1920 (Internet Sacred Texts Archive).

78. *The Cambrian Register*, 1796.

ACKNOWLEDGEMENTS

Thanks are due to the following for permission to use their work and translations:

Erynn Rowan Laurie for 'The Cauldron of Poesy' (see her website under References, no. 58), Andrew Tierney and the Four Courts Press for material taken from *The King of Mysteries*, Janice Manning and Your Own World Books for the quotations from their remarkable *Kolbrin Bible*. John B. Hare, host of the incomparable Internet Sacred Texts Archive (see References) has given me much advice and guidance. The version of 'The Salmon of Knowledge' comes from Celt.org. Despite many attempts, I've been unable to contact the 'Mad Poet' who hosts the site, but I gratefully acknowledge him here.

The author has made every effort to secure permission to reproduce material protected by copyright. He will be pleased to make good any omissions brought to his attention in future printings of this book.